"This book comes at an important time when we need more women in leadership positions. Dr. Lucius has found that intersection between empowering women and improving government through public service." —**Atalie Ebersole, President of Women Under Forty Political Action Committee**

"After reading this book cover to cover, I strongly feel that it will be helpful in healing the current divide between Democrats & Republicans (of which I am neither), and in general prying us loose from our political stereotypes. I am also personally inspired by Casey's journey, lessons, and scars. Reading her story will prove extremely valuable, and incredibly inspiring, for anyone who is facing the challenges of a political campaign." —**Kimberly Wiefling, Author,** *Scrappy Project Management*

"Participating directly in our democracy has never been more important than now. While millions wonder why we have the leaders we do, we welcome the thousands of women who are stepping up at all levels of government to run for office. Dr. Lucius is a courageous candidate with personal experience, intellectual expertise, and an inspirational story to guide the curious on their journey from consideration to candidacy. Be sure to put this book on your must-read list for activists and candidates, especially if you're a conservative." —**Missy Shorey, Executive Director of Maggie's List**

Scrappy Campaigning

10 Things I Learned about Leadership
& Life on the Campaign Trail

By Casey Lucius, PhD
Foreword by Kip Hawley

> *"Watch out for those who cause divisions and put obstacles in your way that are contrary to the teaching you have learned . . . for such people serve their own appetites. By smooth talk and flattery, they deceive the minds of naïve people."*
> *Romans 16:17–18 (57 AD.)*

20660 Stevens Creek Blvd., Suite 210
Cupertino, CA 95014

Published by Happy About®
20660 Stevens Creek Blvd., Suite 210, Cupertino, CA 95014
http://happyabout.com

First Printing: May 2018
Hardcover ISBN: 1-60005-276-2 978-1-60005-276-7
Paperback ISBN: 1-60005-275-4 978-1-60005-275-0
eBook ISBN: 1-60005-277-0 978-1-60005-277-4
Place of Publication: Silicon Valley, California, USA
Paperback Library of Congress Number: 2018937939

Trademarks

Warning and Disclaimer

Meet the Scrappy Guides™

The Scrappy Guides™ is a series of books to help you accomplish the impossible. Those of you who say it can't be done should stay out of the way of those of us doing it!

Scrappy means ATTITUDE.

Scrappy means not relying on a title to be a leader.

Scrappy means being willing to take risks and put yourself out there.

Scrappy means doing the right thing, even when you don't feel like it.

Scrappy means having the steely resolve of a street fighter.

Scrappy means sticking to your guns even if you're shaking in your boots.

Scrappy means being committed beyond reason to a purpose beyond profit and a mission that matters.

Scrappy means being determined to make a positive difference even when you are not positive you can succeed.

Scrappy means caring about something more than you care about being comfortable, socially acceptable, or politically correct.

Scrappy means being absolutely, totally committed to extraordinary results.

Scrappy means EDGY! . . . and is your edge in achieving outrageous results even when they seem impossible.

The Scrappy Guides™ help you muster the courage and commitment to pursue your goals—even when there is no evidence that you can succeed. They are your shield against the naysayers who will try to undermine you, and they will give you comfort during the inevitable failures that accompany most worthy pursuits. When you fail, fail fast, fail forward, in the direction of your goals, lurching fitfully if you must. Sometimes success is built on the foundation of a very tall junk pile.

Let's get scrappy!

The Books in the Scrappy Guides™ Series

Kimberly Wiefling
Scrappy Project Management: *The 12 Predictable and Avoidable Pitfalls Every Project Faces*
土壇場プロジェクト 成功の方程式 単行本
Inspired Organizational Cultures: *Discover Your DNA, Engage Your People, and Design Your Future*

Julie Abrams, Carole Amos, Eldette Davie, Mai-Huong Le, Hannah Kain, Sue Lebeck, Terrie Mui, Pat Obuchowski, Yuko Shibata, Nathalie Udo, Betty Jo Waxman, Kimberly Wiefling
Scrappy Women in Business: *Living Proof That Bending the Rules Isn't Breaking the Law*

Michael Seese
Scrappy Information Security: *The Easy Way to Keep the Cyber Wolves at Bay*
Scrappy Business Contingency Planning: *How to Bullet-Proof Your Business and Laugh at Volcanoes, Tornadoes, Locust Plagues, and Hard Drive Crashes*

Michael Horton
Scrappy General Management: *Common Sense Practices to Avoid Calamities, Catastrophes, and Lackluster Results for Corporations and Small Businesses*

Casey Lucius
Scrappy Campaigning: *10 Things I Learned about Leadership & Life on the Campaign Trail*

Meet the Scrappy Guides™ Executive Editor

SiliconValleyAlliances.com <http://siliconvalleyalliances.com/>
KimberlyWiefling.com <http://kimberlywiefling.com/>
Phone: +1 650 867 0847

Become a Scrappy Guides Author

Have a "Scrappy" streak in you? Want to write about it?
Let's spread the scrappy word together!
As the executive editor of the Scrappy Guides™,
I provide guidance, support, and comic relief!
Contact me and let's talk. Email me at kimberly@wiefling.com
<kimberly@wiefling.com>.

Dedication

To God and His plan.

Acknowledgments

First and foremost, I want to thank my husband, Bob Lucius, for putting up with me. He has been my partner and cheerleader for the past 16 years. He dealt with my late nights when I was on city council, always with a smile, but the real test of our relationship was when I came home and told him I wanted to quit my job and run for Congress. He not only went along with it, but he encouraged me and believed in me. I also have to thank our son, Bobby, who was the star in most of my commercials. He walked door-to-door with me, marched in parades with me, and told everyone we met that his mom was running for office. I could not have undertaken such a challenging endeavor without the support of my husband and my son. Thank you both!

I also want to thank my mom. This is the lady who raised me to be a strong, independent, go-getting, scrappy young woman. She has always been proud of me, and encouraged me every step of the way through my life. When I told her I wanted to run for Congress, she said, "Go big or go home, baby!" Thank you, Mom, for never making me feel like my dreams are silly.

To my team: thank you! Kip, Mike, Laura, Jennifer, Robert, Megan, Ren, Andrew, and Val, I can't thank you enough for taking a year out of your lives to help me run a national campaign in a really tough district. You all are amazing people, and I'm a far better person for knowing you. Thank you to the 1,108 donors who believed in me enough to open up their checkbooks. Whether it was ten bucks or a thousand, your contributions meant the world to me. Some of you also opened your homes to me. Some of you volunteered or sent me notes of encouragement. You know who you are. Thank you!

Finally, thank you to the endlessly scrappy Kimberly Wiefling, who answered my email when I wanted to write this scrappy book. Thank you for the time you spent walking me through the process and editing it. And I truly appreciate my publisher, Mitchell Levy, and the entire Happy About publishing team, for making this book a reality.

Contents

Images

Scrappy Campaigning draws from the experience of a remarkable woman who served our country overseas, both on active duty and as a civilian, and who then came home to embody practical applications of American values. In this book, she shares with us the roller-coaster moments she experienced as she engaged in the core of the democratic process to which she has devoted her life. Casey Lucius running for Congress was an act of patriotism, bravery, and faith. *Scrappy Campaigning* takes us on that journey with her as she shares the lessons learned that come only from running in those shoes. Regardless of party affiliation or political background, anyone interested in campaigning in the US will benefit from reading this book filled with Casey's real-life experiences in public service and politics.

When House Speaker Paul Ryan came to San Francisco in July 2016 to raise money, he stood before an exclusive crowd of potential contributors and . . . introduced Casey Lucius. There were 52 other Republicans running for Congress from California that year, but the Speaker invited only one to his event. Even more of an honor, he chose to give her precious air-time during his remarks. Why? Paul Ryan wanted new blood in Congress, change agents and doers. Casey was, in many ways, the perfect example of that—a veteran, a mom, an experienced elected official, smart, practical, and energetic. So, when a packed house of the power elite shuffled forward in the front room of a mansion with a glorious view of the San Francisco Bay that summer evening to hear Paul Ryan, they also got to hear from Casey. After some introductory remarks of his own, the US Speaker of the House turned and said, "Ladies and gentlemen, Casey Lucius!" And Casey stepped up.

I met Casey the previous year at the beginning of her Congressional campaign, drawn to the same qualities in her that caught the Speaker's attention. I was a constituent, since I live in Pacific Grove where Casey served as a City Council Member, and a 20-year resident of California District 20. I was frustrated that, despite enormous change in the economic and social dynamics of our area, the same closed fraternity of old school political/ business buddies got to pick our elected officials.

The trigger for me was when long-time Congressman Farr announced his retirement. The flock of potential successors who had been patiently and graciously waiting for Farr to retire magically scattered! The credentials of those leaving the race were formidable—a former major city mayor who was a woman, the leader of the Assembly's Hispanic Caucus, the State Senate Majority Leader, and a serving mayor. After they all backed out, the only Democrat running was the son of Farr's predecessor, the iconic Leon Panetta. I vented to my wife in our kitchen as I read about Panetta's announcement, "How can this happen? They just picked him and nobody said a word!" I thought the job was supposed to be elected, not inherited! It felt wrong.

Early in my career, I worked on a Senate staff, and also served in the Reagan Administration in a variety of jobs, including one in charge of Congressional Relations at the Department of Transportation. After a spell as a senior official in the White House, I switched to a business career that lead me to California. After 9/11, I was asked to come back to Washington and lead the creation of the Transportation Security Administration (TSA). A few years later I returned to TSA to be the Administrator until 2009. All this is to say that I have a deep interest in, and somewhat eclectic experience with, the US Congress and the people who inhabit it. So it rankled me that, despite the obvious need for new energy and diversity in the Congress, my own district was a stale political backwater. As I put the paper down on the kitchen table, rant concluded, my patient wife said, "There's a young female Republican running. You ought to read up on her." Indeed!

Casey Lucius is impressive on paper and blows you away in person. I met Casey much the way you readers someday might, one on one over a cup of coffee. We talked about the campaign and who she was. In truth, I had already figured that out, as it was obvious. Casey grew up in modest means and enrolled in the Navy's Officer Candidate School right out of college. She served seven years on active duty as an Intelligence Officer, including on the aircraft carrier *USS Stennis* as one of only a handful of women on this 5,000-crew ship. Casey went on to be the lead intelligence briefer to the Commander of the Pacific Fleet. Hers was not an easy path, and "self-made" jumps off the page when you read about her experiences. Casey decided that she wanted to shape policy and, after earning a master's degree, challenged herself to get a PhD in political science. In the midst of all that, Casey served in our Embassy in Hanoi. When that mission was accomplished, the now "Dr. Lucius" got selected to be a Professor at the Naval War College. Phew! Self-made with a bullet. This is a woman who watched C-SPAN as a kid and used the Star-Spangled Banner as her career guide!

By the time I met her, Casey had added a young son and had been elected to the City Council. Before meeting her to talk about her campaign, I wanted to see Casey in action, so I went to a City Council meeting. You know it when you see it, and Casey Lucius is a natural. Add polish and civic accomplishment to that background of hers, and you have a star. Taking the next step to Congress did not seem like too big of a leap.

In my time in Washington, I got to know dozens of Members of Congress and had seen the inner workings at all levels—from alcoves in the Capitol to the Oval Office. The question I asked myself after meeting Casey was, "Why is this woman not already in some national office?" Apart from the

Paul Ryan wanting new energy in Congress, Casey has rare intangibles. She knows how to deeply listen—to absorb the facts, note the nuances, and read the subtext of what someone tells her. Her questions (and there are always a lot of them) reflect her understanding of, and gently probe, what she hears. Casey is pleasantly relentless in inserting a "therefore" into whatever you are discussing. Once you know her, you come to know that your conversation is not finished until you have agreed upon a specific action item. This is unusual in a public figure. Most people in politics lead by talking. Casey is not driven by hearing herself talk, she is committed to getting concrete things done. I was so motivated by the notion that Casey should be in national politics that I basically took the next year off and worked on her campaign full-time to help make that happen.

Unfortunately, at the conclusion of that year, I was reminded that victory does not always go to the most deserving. Ideas, ideals, and intelligence do not trump embedded local power. And, as you will read in this book, we made some mistakes along our difficult campaign path. Nevertheless, Casey was undaunted, even against stiff odds. She refused to be thrown off when allies wilted or trolls came at her from the shadows. Casey generated buzz wherever she went. It was a revelation, no matter what the issue, to see how a crowd would turn from skeptical . . . to curious . . . to engaged . . . and then riveted, until coming alive with positive energy at the end. This happened at event after event. In every dimension but votes, Casey came out of her Congressional race a winner. And, as a result, she now has a story to tell that we can all learn from.

Just as Casey's remarks at the Speaker's event in San Francisco that night lit up that room, in *Scrappy Campaigning*, Casey Lucius inspires us with this challenge: in order to live in the land of the free, we must first be the home of the brave.

Kip Hawley
Author of *Permanent Emergency:
Inside the TSA and the Fight for the Future*

Casey Lucius and Kip Hawley

1 The Personal Side of Public Service

"I get up every morning both determined to change the world and have one hell of a good time. Sometimes, this makes planning the day difficult."
—*E.B. White*

The Beginning: A Reason to Serve

From the time I was a little girl, I wanted to change the world. When I was 10 years old, I started telling people I was going to be the first woman president. One of my favorite shows was C-SPAN and I desperately wanted to be there on the floor of the Senate with them, debating the merits of this or that policy. This seemed quite ambitious considering that I grew up in an apartment in a small town in Ohio with my mom working two jobs and my step-dad working in a factory. No one in my family had ever run for office, no one had served in the military, and we had no family money or a famous last name. But that never stopped me from dreaming of someday serving in public office . . . and of course, changing the world!

Because of this pull to "serve" from a young age, I ran for the student council when I was in high school and was selected to be the class vice president. I attended college at Ashland University where, as a sophomore, I ran for president of the student senate, winning the race, using the extremely popular slogan: "It's Miller Time! Vote for Casey Miller!" This made me the only sophomore to ever be student senate president. After college, I joined the military and served for seven years on active duty as a Naval Intelligence Officer. This included two glorious years on an aircraft carrier and three years working in the not-so-glorious basement of the Pacific Fleet Headquarters. Regardless of the level of glamour, nothing could pull me away from this work.

Throughout my life, I've always found ways to serve by volunteering in my community, including working for Habitat for Humanity, raising money for the Kairos Coalition, serving on the Board of Directors of Pearl Buck International and Jacob's Heart, and more. In my mind, these were necessary steps to prepare for *real* public service—running for office. Looking back, I realize that volunteering for nonprofits, serving on local committees, and joining the military are all *real* public service, but I maintained my interest and proclivity toward political office. Many people run for office because they have an interest in politics or a specific issue, and some are interested in the fame that comes with that, but most are likely doing so because they want to make a positive difference. Recently, many people feel frustrated by those who are currently in leadership positions, believing that things could be better if only we had different, less self-centered, public leaders. A lot of us want to "do something," but we don't even know where to begin. My political life, such as it is, started with a speed bump—literally, a speed bump!

My husband and I had just bought our first home in Pacific Grove, California, in 2009. This was thrilling because I grew up living in apartments and moving around a lot. The thought of owning a house and settling into a quaint neighborhood was truly the American dream being realized. I was also pregnant with our son at the time, which made this "happy homeowner" experience all the more blissful. Then one day, someone knocked at our door complaining about cars driving too fast and asking me to sign a petition to have a speed bump installed in our neighborhood. It turns out that there was a tricky three-way intersection behind our house, and some of the parents and neighbors found it to be dangerous. They thought a speed bump would help. Fair enough. I signed the petition. The next thing I knew, I was applying to be on the Traffic Safety Commission. You may be wondering how signing a petition led to being nominated to a city commission, but I won't bore you with those details. The bottom line is, I noticed something that needed to be done and I took action.

In case you don't know how commissions like this work, let me briefly explain. Every city and county has about a dozen boards and commissions made up of local residents who take up important local issues and make recommendations to the city council or board of county supervisors. These officials then make the final policy decisions. Becoming a member of one of these advisory councils usually starts with an easy application form available on the city or county website, and the applicants are normally nominated and approved by the mayor or full council. From 2009-2012, I served on the Traffic Safety Commission and the ADA Compliance Committee. Although we only met once a month, contributing in these ways made me feel like I was more a part of our community. It also gave me the opportunity to attend the city council meetings, and even make comments and recommendations during the meetings. I highly recommend that anyone interested in knowing what's going on in your neighborhood should attend a council meeting. They are open to the public, the agendas are posted online in advance, and there is usually time at the beginning or end of each meeting for public comment. Even if you're not interested in running for office, these meetings can be very informative. You'll find out fascinating things like how to get a pothole filled or how to get new books ordered for the library. They can be very entertaining as well!

After participating in the process for a couple of years, in 2012, I decided to run for city council. You see, I had noticed that there was only one woman among the seven council members, and there was no one under the age of 60. Since I was 36 at the time, I figured I could simultaneously double the number of women on the council and drop the average age a few years by joining them. As a new mom and a new homeowner, I had new priorities like investments in our parks, family-oriented recreational activities, public meetings that were accessible to people who worked during the day, and more women and younger people making decisions for the future of our town. Thanks to a successful campaign, I had the opportunity to sit on the city council for four years representing the citizens of Pacific Grove, which I did with honor.

I loved being on the city council, but my call to serve kept nagging me, and by 2016, I found myself in another race. This time, it was much bigger, and much more of a commitment. I ran for the US House of Representatives. I know what you're thinking, it's a mighty jump from city council to the US House, but my opponent had never even served in a local elected office, so he was making an even bigger leap. He did have one advantage, however, as he happened to have a famous father who had been the Director of the CIA, the former Secretary of Defense, and Chief of Staff to President Clinton. This surely made his leap to national office much easier, and probably made his campaign experience quite a bit different from my own. At this point, you may be wondering, "why should I read a book about campaigning from a candidate who didn't even win her race?" Fair question! Running for office and campaigning are not merely about the final outcome. This book is meant for people who want to get involved, but don't know how. It's for people who have a desire to serve, but don't have big money or a famous last name. And it's for people who simply aren't prepared for the obstacles that are inherent in a political campaign. This book isn't about winning or losing, it's about running the race and being prepared for the challenges that will be thrown at you. It's about jumping in, avoiding as many pitfalls as possible, facing the political machine with courage and conviction, and—most importantly— leaving our cities, counties, states, and our country, in a better condition than we found them.

Unlike other campaign books that talk about yard signs, advertising, mailers, and how to get-out-the-vote, this book provides both my personal story and the practical steps required to run a successful campaign while avoiding some of the dangers that no one ever talks about. While many of us feel baffled by politics, we can and must get involved! There are many ways to serve and contribute in a meaningful way, and I hope that my experience will inspire you to do so at whatever level you wish to get involved.

In the following chapters, I'll share in detail the important lessons learned from both my local and national campaign experiences. Together, we'll explore everything from my personal desire to serve and the practical implementation of the campaign, to the reality of running right into a political brick wall. What happens when you are doing everything right, following your well-thought-out campaign plan, but get hit right in the face by the political machine? We'll delve into the role of political parties, money, the media, and the overall intimidation often associated with political campaigns. How can you overcome what you can't control? The short answer is that you can overcome anything if you are properly prepared. This book will prepare you to be scrappy in the face of the seemingly overwhelming odds against you.

It is my hope that this book will encourage you to take a stand, have courage, focus on substance, and keep pressing on in spite of those odds. At the end of the day, our cities, counties, states, and our country will always need good, smart, thoughtful people to run for office. We cannot and *must* not throw up our hands and imagine that it's useless to even try to make a difference. We can do our part to make the issues substantive again, to bring independent thought back into the debate, and make our votes more valuable than money.

Are you ready for public service? Public service is just that—it's public! Your entire life, as well as your family drama, all become public when you run for office. It is, in fact, very personal. A campaign will easily consume a year of your life, and you will miss important times with your family and friends. You'll have to make concessions on issues that you feel strongly about. You will lose debates, lose endorsements, lose money, and you will probably lose some of your mind along the way. It can be risky to put yourself, your family, and your beliefs and ideas on display in front of the entire world. You will definitely be criticized. You will certainly be challenged. But it's okay, as long as you know why you're running this race. You'll need a pretty darn good reason to go through all of this, and I believe that this is where a deep desire for public service will come in handy. Win or lose, a passion to serve will carry you across the finish line. It will carry you through the tough times and sustain you through the ups and downs, especially when you're ready to quit.

You will be asked why you want to run for office, and of course there will be particular issues that you want to address. But because public service is so demanding, you must also have a deeper, more meaningful answer for this inevitable question. For me, I started my run for city council with the strong conviction that every decision-making body should be diverse. It should include women, men, people of color, young, and old, because diverse groups produce superior results. Each person has a valuable perspective and a unique contribution to make. None of us win when we are ruled by old white men, including the old white men! (I'm sorry to the "old white men," because I know and respect a lot of them, but enough is enough.) It's in everyone's best interest for the existing paradigm to change and make room for a new generation, for people with different backgrounds and belief systems, and for women. This strongly held belief led me to embark on my US Congressional race as well. The House seat had been held by the same man for 23 years. He was a man of public service who I admired and respected. Even though we were from different political parties, I agreed with him on many issues. I simply did not believe, and still don't, that any elected seat should be monopolized by the same person for decades. In fact, in that district, that seat had been held by only two men in the past 40 years. In my view, it was time for a change—for a woman, for a new generation, for someone with a middle-class background, and for fresh ideas. My belief in the American Dream also pushed me toward this challenge. I believe that, in this great country, you can set your sights on any goal and—if you work hard—you can make any dream a reality. (Luck is also helpful, of course!) At that time, I also believed that anyone can run for office and be successful. If I didn't believe that, I wouldn't have written this book. After all, my favorite movie is still *Mr. Smith Goes to Washington*! Some people might call me naïve, but I don't think you have to have a lot of money or a famous last name to make a difference. I don't support the idea that only the rich can contribute to society. I strongly believe that we are a country of opportunity . . . for everyone . . . no matter where you come from . . . and I put this theory to the test in my own campaign. And precisely *because* I won one election and lost another, I am convinced that this is the greatest country on Earth, that we do have a government *of* the people and *by* the people, and will continue to enjoy all that this country makes possible as long as people like you and I are willing to step up and run for office.

Now let's get busy!

2 The Practical Side of Public Service

"In war, you can only be killed once, in politics, many times." —Winston Churchill

---

Lesson 1: Know Where Your Money Is Coming From

When I ran for city council in 2012, I campaigned for nine months and raised just over $5,000. Less than four years later, I ran for Congress, spent 17 months campaigning, and raised nearly half a million dollars. I worked hard for every cent! Throughout the process, money was the most important element of both campaigns. Initially, I didn't want to admit this, but I quickly realized that the amount of money raised is strongly correlated to how credible the candidate appears, as well as how many people believe that candidate can win. It also impacts whether you can hire a staff, buy advertising, rent a campaign office, purchase data, or even file the paperwork required to get your name on the ballot. Yes, unfortunately, it all comes down to money. Honestly, when I read that in other campaign books, I would think, "Well, that won't apply to me! I'll focus on the issues! I'll be a breath of fresh air! I'll just ask for votes rather than money." If you're thinking this way, let me save you a few steps and a lot of heartache. Just accept the fact that money is required in any political race—usually a whole bunch of it.

My first, and probably most important, piece of advice is to form a finance committee. This committee should be made up of five to 10 individuals who commit to raising a certain amount of money for your campaign. For example, if you are running for a local office, you may ask each person to raise $500. Contribution caps are often established by cities and counties, but it is realistic to ask 10 people who believe in your campaign, and who want to see you get elected, to raise $500 each. This could consist of a single donation from that committee member, or they could persuade five people to donate $100 each.

In a larger state or national race, you might ask your finance committee members to raise $20,000 each. In a national race, the contribution limit is $2,700 per person per election. This means someone can donate $2,700 for your primary race and then another $2,700 for the general election, a total of $5,400 per person.[1] Now, I don't personally know a lot of people who can write a check for $5K, but the idea of having a finance committee is that those individuals should know at least a few people who can write those kinds of checks. If one person on your finance committee gets four people to make the maximum donation, they bring in $21,600 to your campaign. If you have a half dozen or so people on your committee who can achieve this, you'll bring in over $100K. Not bad!

If you are considering running for office or working on a campaign, you need to draft a campaign plan. Going through this planning process will give the candidate, her family, and close confidants time to envision what this campaign would actually look like. What would the timeframe be? How much money should be raised? What issues will be the main focus of the campaign? What staff positions should be paid? Which should be volunteer? And there are many more questions that will be inspired by this crucial planning process. There are a number of great books and even free samples online detailing campaign plans, so I won't rehash that here, but while writing the campaign plan is the time to think deeply about who should be on your finance committee.

The next step is to sit down with these individuals and ask them to commit their precious time to help you raise money. These relationships can be tricky, because sometimes people working on your campaign will want to give you advice about what to say to the media, or what position to take

---

[1] Check with the FEC because contribution limits may change.

on a particular issue. Naturally, you can listen to their comments, but that is not the role of the people on your finance committee.

Think of six leaders in the community who will believe in your candidacy and can help you raise money, then meet with them to make the case for why they should be on your team. Let them know that you're working on a campaign plan and a staffing plan in order to ensure that you have all the right people in place to help with debate prep and writing press releases. But emphasize that where you really need help is in meeting donors and influential people in the community, and this is where they come in. Make it clear up front that each person will be asked to raise X amount, and share with them who else you're considering for the finance committee. If you have no idea who these individuals should be, think about local business owners representing different industries, perhaps the mayor and other locally elected officials, and someone in the party leadership. These are the folks most likely to have money and know people who have money. If you know someone who has already been elected, they can identify potential donors based on who donated to their campaign. Someone on the county or state party central committee will also know local donors who donate to the party, and they will know how to reach them. Pay special attention to business owners. Think about having a leader in each of the agricultural, medical, automobile, hospitality, high-tech, and banking industries. There is a two-fold benefit to getting the support of business owners: not only can they help you raise money, they can also secure important endorsements from other leaders who work in their sector.

Now you may be thinking that all you have to do is put together the right finance committee and—poof!—they will go out and magically raise money for you, leaving you free to study the issues and make commercials. Not so! Ideally, your committee will bring in some significant donations, but it's likely that they will deliver only about half of what you need. The other half will be up to you. It's hard to know exactly how much you'll need to run an effective campaign, but you can get a good estimate by looking at past campaign records in your city or county. This information is publicly available, and you can easily find the financial reports of those currently in office, as well as those who have run in previous campaigns.

Prior to running for city council, I spoke to several former council members and asked how much they raised in their own races. Most of them gave me an estimate of $5K, so that became my benchmark. In my Congressional race, I started out running against an incumbent who had been in office for over two decades. Looking over his campaign finance reports, I saw that he usually raised around $700,000 for every election. The reports provided the overall total, as well as a list of expenses. This gave me a good idea of how much I would need to raise, and how that money would likely be allocated.

In my experience, there are three main ways that you can raise money: 1) hire a professional fundraiser who will introduce you to "bundlers," basically paid money-raisers; 2) hire a fundraising company that will sell you lists of past donors and their contact information; 3) dial and smile . . . in other words, call people yourself and ask for money. I'll share some of the pros and cons of each of these approaches. Spoiler alert: the only approach that worked for me was option #3—I had to pick up the phone and just ask for donations.

Let's start with the people in the political world known as "bundlers." They go out and raise money and "bundle" it for the candidate. In other words, instead of having the candidate go out and meet 50 people and ask them to each contribute, the bundler would make 50+ phone calls and collect the contributions from each person. This is an amazing gift because one of the hard things about asking for donations is not the initial phone call, it's the five follow-up calls required until the donor actually sends the check! It's extremely time consuming to make these calls, track who you have called, stay on top of who you need to follow up with, and ensure you have all the required information from the donor for reporting purposes. Imagine instead, having a bundler who delivers $300K to your campaign and hands over all the reporting documents to your treasurer! Wow, I can't even imagine it—probably because I never had this person on my campaign team. One of the reasons I didn't have a "bundler" is that I don't know many people who can write a big check, nor do I know people who know people who can write big checks. If this is the case with you, then congratulations! You are running a scrappy campaign! The good news is that you can hire a fundraising company, or professional fundraiser, who knows bundlers all over the nation who do this every campaign season. Bundlers work mostly on Senate and Presidential campaigns, but who knows, there might be a bundler out there who is just looking for the right scrappy candidate to get behind! If you do hire a professional fundraiser to match you with a bundler, they will usually charge a monthly fee, as well as a percentage of whatever money is brought in. Yeah, I know, it's not the ideal version of democracy I imagined as a little girl when I dreamed of running for president either, but that's how the system works. Maybe we should call it "democrazy"!

The closest thing that I had to a bundler was one man, Bill Warner, who had heard me speak at an in-home "meet and greet." He liked what I had to say, and he became a great advocate for my campaign. Not only did he and his wife make a significant donation, but they also hosted an event in their home for me where I was able to meet other large donors and make my case to them. He also introduced me to another person who offered to host an in-home fundraiser. These events enabled me to tell my story and make my case for why the attendees should both vote for me and donate to my campaign. The extra step that Bill took was to continue to introduce me to potential donors throughout my campaign, including personally making calls to them to ask them for money. His efforts alone probably helped me raise over $40,000! That's the power of one influential person who believes in you.

In my campaign, every penny mattered, so I didn't feel comfortable paying a monthly fee to a professional fundraiser without knowing how much they could actually bring in. If you decide to hire a company or an individual, definitely do your research so you know exactly what you are paying for. Also, ask for references and call those references to investigate their fundraising track record. Be clear in the contract about how much you expect them to bring in, and set the monthly fee or percentage based on those expectations. For example, you might stipulate that no monthly fee will be paid until the first $10,000 is raised, from $10,000–$100,000, the campaign will pay 15% with no monthly fee, or 10% with X monthly fee. Yes, everything is negotiable, but these companies do get a lot of business during election years, so you probably need them more than they need you.

By the way, even a professional fundraiser will ask you how much money you've raised on your own. When I was asked this by one company, I wanted to say, "Hey buddy, that's why I'm hiring you!" But that won't fly because they also need to demonstrate to their donors that you are a credible candidate, and the best way to do that is to say, "She's already raised $150,000 on her own and gotten significant endorsements from . . ." You get the picture.

While I didn't hire a bundler to help me raise money, I was introduced to a professional fundraiser I met in San Francisco (outside of my district). He introduced me to larger donors and potential bundlers, and that was a partial success. Those I met in person made donations, usually the maximum amount. However, I never did meet a bundler, or have any luck getting those individual donors to become bundlers on my behalf. Yes, I got a few extra donations out of the deal, but by the time I calculated the fees owed to the fundraiser, as well as my time traveling to meet these donors, I'm not sure it was worth it. Another consideration when meeting people outside of your district is whether or not it's worth meeting with donors who can't even vote for you. On the one hand, each time I got a $5,000 donation, I could purchase a 30-second commercial on TV, which would certainly reach thousands of potential voters in my district. On the other hand, spending the entire day in the car driving to and from a meeting with one person is time that could have been spent meeting with local donors and voters. It's a tough trade off.

In the end, it comes down to how much money you need to raise overall and how much time you have to raise it. Hopefully, your campaign plan has a budget and timeline so you're not just guessing at the numbers. Someone once recommended that if I needed to raise $500,000 and I had one year to do it, I should take the number of days in the year (minus holidays, occasions like my son's birthday, and family vacation, etc.) and divide the total money I needed to raise by the number of days remaining in the year. For example, say that there are 275 days left in the year that you can call people and ask for money, and you need to raise $500K. This means that you should plan on raising $1,820 each and every day. If one meeting with a donor eats up your entire day, it's worth it, as long as they write you check for over $1,820. If you leave that meeting with no check, then the next day, you'll need to raise $3,640 to be on track! You can also break down your daily fundraising goal by the hour (but that's a bit obsessive, don't you agree?) or by the week, but daily is probably most effective. If you want to do the hourly thing, consider that you can't really call people and ask them for money before 9:00 am and you can't call during the dinner hour. You really have only eight hours a day to either meet with or make phone calls to donors, which means that each hour, you need to raise about $228. I made a lot of phone calls to friends and neighbors who agreed to donate $25 or $50. At this rate, I had to talk to about nine people every hour. A lot of people don't answer their phones anymore, so sometimes I had to call 30 numbers an hour to speak to nine people! That's 30 numbers every hour for eight hours straight. Try it sometime! It's a marathon. Thank goodness for those rare $5,000 checks that bought me some time during the day or even freed up an entire day for me to focus on other important aspects of the campaign.

In some situations, it's helpful to break down your fundraising goal by the hour. As a candidate, I was often invited to speak at a women's luncheon or Rotary luncheon. These are terrific opportunities to get in front of 50 to 100 voters, but these events can often take two hours out of your day, so if you can't walk out of there with two times your hourly target, you might decide not to go. Similarly, if you call someone to ask for a donation and they want to meet you for coffee or lunch to discuss specific issues, consider going only if you're sure that you will raise your hourly target. I know, it seems harsh, but you can always have coffee with them after you're elected!

If you don't want to go the bundling route because you are looking for smaller donations from more people rather than larger donations from a few people, another option is to hire a fundraising company that will sell you lists of donors. This may also answer that nagging question in the back of your mind, "If I have to call 30 people every hour for eight hours, five days per week, holy cow, that's 1,200 people! How do I get the names and phone numbers of all the people I'll have to call?" Well, here you go. There are lists of previous donors from all over the US comprised of people who have donated to either the national Republican party or the national Democratic party, and also of those who have donated in local, state, or national elections. Once someone donates to any campaign, their name, phone number, mailing address, and often their email address become public information. Companies scour the internet and the public records within each secretary of state's office to compile this information and sell it to candidates. Candidates can buy lists of only Republican or only Democratic donors, or they can buy lists of donors that live in a specific zip code. Lists of donors based on a specific issue—people who feel passionately about abortion or national security (some companies do this level of analysis and will also sell you such data)—can also be purchased. Pricing is usually per name. For example, if you want a list of 10,000 past donors, it may cost ten cents per name ($1,000) plus a percentage of the donations received based on that list. (Okay, the fundraising company doesn't actually give you a list, they just agree to contact people on the list for you. Simultaneously, they're also doing this for other candidates. This explains why you get so many random emails from all over the country asking you to donate money during election years.) I bought a US-wide list of donors, and my campaign team drafted an email solicitation to send to people on that list. We then sent the fundraising company our solicitation email, and they sent it out to the potential donors. Because I was a member of a particular party, our email was worded to appeal to other members of that party, and we asked them to donate a specific amount of money rather than to simply donate. Here is a sample of one of our email blasts.

CASEY LUCIUS
★ ★ FOR CONGRESS ★ ★

We are gaining momentum!
Every dollar counts! Your contributions have helped us raise over $375,000!

The response from the debate last week has been overwhelming! Thank you!

With your help we were able to exceed our online fundraising goal of $5,000 before the FEC deadline three days ago!

Our hard work has landed this race as one of the top races that Fox News will be watching through this last month of the election. Last night, Sunday October 2nd, Fox News aired a segment about this race!

Bret Bair said, "There are many interesting races across the nation...one of those races is in California where the son of a political icon is going up against a new face of the Republican party."

Click Here to watch the clip aired on Fox News Channel last night!
If you have not had a chance to watch the debate check it out Here!

We need your help!

My opponent is funded by special interests and PACS.

Please donate now to help us battle politics as usual!

Donate $100 Now

If someone does donate through the fundraising company via these email blasts, it will go through their online system. They will deduct their cut and send you a check for the remainder. I'm not sure exactly how many emails were actually sent out for my campaign via this effort, but the most that was ever raised was around $500. Now, you could say that was $500 I didn't have before, but it actually took quite a lot of time to negotiate the fundraising contract, draft the emails, coordinate the timing of the emails to be sent, and receive the money. More annoyingly, the company sent us the donations, but they failed to send all of the information that my treasurer needed for reporting. You see, every donor to a political campaign has to be reported, even if you're only running for a city council seat. At a minimum, you are required to report the name, address, amount donated, and occupation of the donor. Having a fundraising company transfer a measly $500 into your account is not really helpful without a report containing all of the relevant and legally required donor information. My treasurer spent way too much time sorting this all out. In the end, sending emails to random people outside of my district just wasn't worth the hassle. If you choose to go this route, thoroughly research the fundraising companies, ask about their procedures, and make sure that you have a main point of contact for questions or concerns. Get references and call around to make sure the company is both reputable and successful.

So, what is the best way to raise money? Call people and ask for a donation. Simple, right? Not so much. But it does work, and I'm a firm believer that it is the best and fastest way to fund your campaign. And when you are making these phone calls, there are three things you should ask any potential donor. First, ask them for their support (i.e., ask them to vote for you). Second, ask them for a donation, and suggest a specific amount. Third, ask them for the names of three family members or friends that you could call as well.

Asking for someone's vote is pretty easy, especially if you believe in what you're doing and why you're doing it. You might start out by explaining why you're running for office and what you hope to accomplish. Go through it quickly because the reason for your call is to get a donation, not to spend time chatting. Remember, you have eight more people to call in that hour! You also shouldn't get into specific issues with people. If they ask your position on an issue, definitely answer honestly, but generally, it's better to stick to your big picture story: you are running for State Representative (or whatever) because you want a business-friendly climate, and you would be honored to have their vote. Here is a sample script that I used to help me stay on point during these phone calls:

> **Draft Phone Script – Three Asks**
>
> Hi Jeanne, this is Casey Lucius calling and you may know that I'm running for Congress. There hasn't been a change in our representative here for over 23 years and I believe it's time for new blood and new ideas. I would really like to tell you about my campaign and ask you for your vote. (pause and hopefully, they agree).
>
> Part of my campaign strategy requires that I raise $450,000 to be competitive in this district. So far, I've raised $160,000. I'm so grateful to all the people in our community who have donated, and I would like to ask you for a donation of $100. (pause and hopefully, they agree). You can mail a check (give address) or donate online at (give website).
>
> I really appreciate your support and I want to ask one more favor of you. Can you give me the names and phone numbers of three friends or family members who share our values and who I can also call to seek their support? (get your notepad ready so you can write down names and numbers).
>
> I will keep you posted on the campaign via email (get email address) and if you have any questions for me, please call me (give them your personal number or a campaign number). Thank you!

There is actual research on this approach that proves that getting someone to agree to one thing increases the likelihood that they will agree to the next thing. According to Amanda Palmer in *The Art of Asking*, by asking someone to do something and getting them to agree, you create both inertia and a connection. You can then tap into that personal connection, as well as the inertia to ask for what you really want. It's easy to create an instant connection by asking someone to vote for you. Then, build on that positive inertia to ask for their financial support. Also, asking someone to do a favor for you makes it more likely that you will win them over. Scientists found that when someone does a favor for you, they are likely to rationalize that you must have been worth it, and they therefore decide they must like you.[2] Any other conclusion would indicate that they showed bad judgment in doing you a favor. So, if you can get them to agree to vote for you, then you are more likely to convince them to donate. At least at this point, they will have decided that they like you and would have an open mind. Plus, by agreeing to vote for you, they have already indicated that they want you

---

[2]Gregory Myers, "10 Psychology Tricks You Can Use to Influence People," Science Online, Feb 3, 2013.

to win, and you can only win if you have enough money to run a decent campaign. Next step: ask for money!

Many people advised me to always ask for the maximum donation, but I knew that most of the people I was calling were not able to write a check for $2,700, let alone $5,400. Instead, I would typically ask for $1,000 or $100. You may be thinking that there's a big difference between $1,000 and $100, and you'd be right. Here's how I decided which to ask for: if someone had never donated to a campaign (at least to my knowledge), I'd call them, tell them I was running for office and why I thought the race was important. I would then ask for their vote, and next, ask them to mail a check for $100 to my campaign. Finally, I would ask them for the names and phone numbers of three of their friends or family members who shared their values and might be interested in supporting my campaign as well. My hope was that this $100 phone call would turn into $400 by this approach. Of course, I asked their family and friends for their referrals as well!

On the other hand, when calling someone who was a past donor to local, county, or state campaigns, I would ask for $1,000. My logic was that if someone had never donated to a campaign, being asked to donate a large amount the first time could be a real turn off. However, if someone is used to making donations, they might appreciate a candidate who isn't asking them to break the bank, but rather just to make an initial investment. I would also ask for their vote on these thousand-dollar calls and for the three contact referrals, but I'd also add, "I'm asking you for $1,000 now, and I am going to demonstrate to you over the next few months that I'm a serious and credible candidate. Then I'm going to call you back and ask for another $1,000!" Usually, the person on the other end of the phone would laugh, but I was dead serious, and I always followed up to ask for another check. Some of my donors joked that I was stalking them! I didn't care, as long as they kept donating. The good news is, if someone donates once, whether it be $25, $100, or more, they're more likely to donate again. The moment someone makes a donation, they have skin in the game and they want to see you succeed. They become your biggest cheerleaders, and they'll likely keep the donations coming, as long as you keep proving yourself and making progress in your campaign. During my Congressional campaign, I had one lady who I never met, Pam Davis, who donated $10 eight times over the course of my campaign! There was also Tom Winant, who donated $100 thirteen times, and Don Chapin, who donated $1,000 five times during the same campaign. These repeat donations were incredibly surprising to me! On average, about 13%–15% of my donors made more than one contribution. I now realize that in a scrappy campaign, you may not get a lot of big checks, but it is extremely meaningful when you get repeated smaller donations from true believers.

Naturally, your supporters may hesitate to give you names and phone numbers of their family members or friends, but human behavior plays a big role in this. According to psychology research, there is a tactic known as the "door in the face" approach. Basically, it means that you already expect the person to say "no" to your request and slam the door in your face, so one way to make them say "yes" is to ask them for two different things, one of which is difficult to say yes to, and one that's easy to agree to. For example, if you ask them to campaign door-to-door for you, they are likely to turn you down, but if you then ask them to put a sign in their yard or give you a friend's name and phone number, they'll likely feel bad for refusing your first request and will feel obliged to help you out with the second. When you're making your phone calls, even if someone does not agree to make a donation, you should still ask for three contacts. They will likely give you a couple of contacts, and you'll have a chance to get donations from them.

With each phone call, you'll be asking for these three things. Don't hang up without getting at least one of them! And if you get one, you can keep them on your call list and follow up a month later. At that time, update them on your progress and once again ask for a donation and their three contact referrals. Some people may be annoyed by this, but most people will appreciate your persistence. You can even remind them that your persistence is an indication of how hard you will work for them once you're elected!

It's really important throughout the campaign to collect email addresses from people you meet or call. This makes it possible to keep them up to date on how the campaign is going, the progress you're making, and of course, ask them for money. As I stated above, I'm not a big believer in raising money through emails, but there is a difference between sending thousands of random messages to people you don't even know and sending monthly newsletters or email updates to people who live in your district, who have met you, and who agreed to be on your mailing list. Keep in touch with these people! They are your base.

At the beginning of both my local and my national campaign, I sent monthly email updates to my subscribers. I used Mailchimp for this, but there are also several other useful services for sending bulk emails that you might find helpful. Don't try to use Yahoo or a free service. These will send your email directly to the recipients' spam box. And be careful not to ask for money in every email because people will just start deleting the emails without even reading them. Something to consider including is a catchy subject line so recipients will want to open and read your email. One of my email blasts was titled, "Campaign Poem for 2016." It was sent out on New Year's Eve and read:

Oh the places we'll go
Oh the people we'll see
But before the journey begins
There's a few things we'll need

Some sneakers to wear
To walk door-to-door
Some fliers in hand
Yard signs and more

With Casey shirts on
We'll man farmer's markets
Smiling and waving
Registered voters our targets

In this campaign we'll have a real blast
We'll surprise everyone and kick some . . .
But before you toast and make your resolution
Ring in the New Year with a small contribution!

If you donate now
I will make you a deal
No more poems will I write
No more spam in your email.

Enjoy the New Year
And don't be like me
With my family in bed at 9PM will I be.
We'll drink apple juice to toast the New Year
I wish you all a fun time full of laughs and great cheer!

It's important to have some fun with these emails. Keep things light, not just in your correspondence but throughout the campaign. Show your supporters that you have a great sense of humor. Use any opportunity you can to reveal your humanity, laugh, and allow others to laugh with you (or even at you!). Another useful part of your emails to supporters, especially when you are asking for a contribution, is to tell them exactly how you plan to spend their money. Here's an example:

> March 31 is the end of the filing period. We have two days to meet our fundraising goals. This month we had the following expenses:
>
> 250 yard signs cost $1,450
> Candidate filing cost $1,740
> Candidate statement in the voter guide: $10,164
>
> Help us make up these costs by making a contribution today! Thank you!

As the campaign went on, we sent these emails more frequently and provided specific dates that were important, including filing deadlines, upcoming debates, press interviews, and volunteer events, as well as significant endorsements and media exposure. The idea was to create a sense of urgency so people would feel compelled to donate right away, and to reassure them about how their money would be spent to further our campaign objectives. Of course, most people won't read your email, but your consistent supporters will, and this communication lifeline is vital to maintaining their trust in you.

During the primary, I had a campaign advisor who told me not to spend any money on the primary. He advised me to save my money for the general election because that was the one that really mattered. Just prior to the primary, my opponent was spending tens of thousands of dollars on TV advertising so his face was all over TV, while I was nowhere in sight. One local business owner, an owner of a few McDonald's franchises, asked to meet with me. He expressed his frustration that he was seeing my opponent on TV every morning but never seeing me. I told him about our strategy of saving money for the general election. He didn't like that strategy and asked how much it would take to get me on television ASAP. I didn't really know, but I did know that the most he could donate was $5.4K, so I asked him for the maximum donation. He wrote me a check for $5,400 on the spot in exchange for my commitment to make a commercial and get on TV as soon as possible. And that's exactly what I did. With that money, I was able to produce a TV ad and secure several 30-second spots during primetime the week prior to the primary election. There were five candidates running in this race: one Republican, one Democrat, and three Independents. I'm happy to say that I made it through the primary, and I think that TV ad made all the difference.

Another way to get donations is through in-home meet-and-greets or personal fundraisers where individuals offer to host an event in their homes. Some of these were quite successful, like when I met Bill Warner, but most were not. Many of these events were terrific opportunities for me to meet voters, but they were not successful fundraisers. It's still worthwhile to do these kinds of things, but they are time-consuming, both for the candidate and the person hosting. And you will most likely walk away with very little money. All things considered, if you secure just a few small donations, it's pretty much a bust. The best thing to do when someone offers to host a coffee meeting or taco party is to tell them exactly what your fundraising goals are. You could say, "I have to raise $10,000 a week to stay on track, so I would need this event to bring in half of that to be worth both of our time. Is that possible?" If someone from your church offers to have a group of ladies over for coffee to meet you, you are not likely to raise $5,000 from that event. Instead you may be better off proposing that the ladies come and hear you speak at an event that is already scheduled on a specific date. However, if the CEO of the community hospital offers to host evening drinks and invite his colleagues, you should take advantage of his offer. Of course, you should still let him know what your fundraising goals are, and be clear about your expectations for the event, but it's more likely that you'll achieve your goal at that event than at the church social. If you're really scrappy, you could even ask, "Would you mind if I invite a few ladies from my church?" Try to combine events. It can be exhausting to go to a different person's house every night of the week in order to make your pitch, and it can become extremely disheartening if those events don't result in some cash to keep your campaign afloat.

Speaking of making your pitch, here's an important lesson that I learned about what really resonates with people. Unfortunately, it took me too long to figure out that people cast their vote based on issues, but they often donate based on personal connection. I spent a lot of time early in my campaigns talking about issues. I like talking about policy because I feel confident studying policy positions, staking out a position, and taking a stand. I could easily make my case for a particular policy position in front of any group, and I could hold my own in any debate on the issues. But I finally realized that this doesn't help you raise money. Over time, I learned that what really resonated with people was when I shared my personal story and my personal reasons for running for office. The truth was, I wasn't running for office because of immigration or water or any other policy issue, I was running for office because I felt I needed to serve in some meaningful way and add some new blood and diversity in our district. When I shifted to sharing my personal story from the heart, people felt a personal connection to me. They felt that I was genuine, and they wanted to help me. Here's the story that I shared:

I grew up living in apartments in Ohio, and my mom often worked two jobs to support our family. She worked as a secretary during the day and she worked at a car dealership in the evenings. My step-dad, Ernie worked in a factory. We lived paycheck to paycheck and there wasn't ever any money left over after paying for the essentials. I knew that I wanted a different life for myself. I knew I wanted to go to college, but I also realized that it would be difficult for my parents to afford.

One day I was sitting at the kitchen table, with college applications spread out on the table in front of me. Even the application fee was out of reach. My mom, who was standing at the kitchen sink, turned to me and said, "You can't go. We can't afford it." I remember putting my head on the table and crying and thinking "This is it! I'm going to be stuck here forever. I'm going to be a waitress, living in apartments my entire life." To make a long story short, my step-dad, Ernie stepped up. He offered to cash in part of his retirement to help me pay for college. It was still a struggle and I still waited tables all through college, but he and my mom made that sacrifice for me. They believed in me and they stepped up when I needed them.

What I learned from that experience was to step up when I'm needed. When there's something I can contribute, I'd better take action and make that contribution. When there's an opportunity for me to make a positive difference, I'd better not squander that opportunity. So now, in this election, I'm stepping up. I quit my cushy job as a professor and threw my hat in the ring for this campaign because we need fresh ideas, we need new solutions to our problems. I'm stepping up for this district like Ernie stepped up. And now, I need each of you to step up and support me.

Usually, you could hear a pin drop after I told this story. And sometimes there were tears, including my own. It wasn't a message about politics or controversial issues, it was about what we all need to do to make our communities a better place. It was genuine and heartfelt, and people connected with this message and with me. Afterward, I would take questions. Then I would talk about the issues if necessary, but most importantly, I told people that I needed their help, that I needed them to donate, to tell their friends and neighbors about me, to put up a yard sign or volunteer on the campaign. This was the perfect time to capture the hearts and minds of my audience and convince them to step up!

Let me wrap up this chapter with a cautionary tale. It's a story about one donor who wrote me a large check and hosted an event, but ultimately turned out to be a nightmare. A retired doctor, he was respected in the community, so when he invited me to his house where I went to meet him, I was eager to tell him about my campaign. I went alone, which no candidate should ever do. It's not wise for a female candidate to visit donors alone, where they could be exploited for money, the money they are asking for. Even for male candidates, I also caution them to be mindful about meeting people alone because someone may be posing as a donor when really, they want to do harm to the candidate. At the end of our initial meeting, he gave me a check for $1,000. At this point, everything appeared fine. After a month or so, I followed up with him and asked him for $4,000 more. Part of the reason that I asked for such a large amount was because he had been calling me regularly to ask about my progress or my positions on the issues, and he seemed very interested in my success. He invited me back to his home for a second visit and gave me a check for $4,000. Then he also offered to host an event and invite a lot of his doctor friends. I thought I had hit the jackpot! On the day of the event, my husband and son, my friend Betty, and I all showed up a bit early to get things set up and be prepared when the guests arrived. No one was there! There were no caterers and no food or drinks set out. I asked the host what we could help with and he assured me that everyone was coming, and that food was going to be delivered shortly. Another hour went by and no one came. I should have left by now, but I didn't. Eventually, a few friends started to straggle in. Still no food appeared and not a single drink was offered, not even water! Over the next hour or so, about 10 or 12 people arrived. And then finally, someone showed up with some sandwiches, praise God, because I was "hangry" (hungry + angry) by this point! I made the best of it by mingling and making my pitch to the individual guests, but I think I only got one donation from that event. To the host, it all seemed perfectly normal. I guess I wasn't clear on what a candidate meet-and-greet should look like, or how much money I expected to raise from such an event. Needless to say, this was a complete waste of time.

Unfortunately, the story doesn't end there. This retired doctor later offered to donate more money. He had already given the maximum (or close to it), but he wanted his adult children to make maximum donations as well, so he invited me over and gave me three checks for $5K each, one from each of his children. When I gave the checks to my treasurer, he wouldn't accept them. Thank goodness I had a treasurer who was both knowledgeable about election law and extremely ethical. He told me that each person had to sign the check and provide their own address and occupation. I told the doctor this, so he invited me back during the Christmas holiday to meet his adult children and get the necessary information. You might be getting the picture by now that he enjoyed inviting me to his home. By this time, I was starting to feel very uncomfortable with the situation. This time when I visited him, I took a friend with me. My friend happens to be a half-black, half-Asian female. When we got to the house, none of his kids were there, so we waited and made small talk. After a few minutes, he asked to speak to me privately in the kitchen, where he proceeded to tell me that if I wanted his money, my friend needed to get out of his house and have nothing more to do with my campaign. He was visibly angry, and I was in complete shock! Did he just tell me to ditch my friend . . . my friend of seven years, who has been one of my biggest supporters? I calmly said, "Cynthia doesn't work on my campaign, but she is my friend, and she will always be my friend." He grabbed the checks out of my hand, ripped them in half, and yelled, "Then get out!"

Cynthia and I walked out of the house and got into my car. I didn't say anything until we were well out of sight of his house. When I told her what had happened, we both started crying. We were both mad and sad. Cynthia has experienced discrimination before, so she was less shocked than I was, but she was much angrier, and I was completely heartbroken for my friend. I had just been hit in the face with the reality that even in 2016, black and brown people still face this kind of discrimination every single day. And now it had seeped into my campaign, from a large, well-educated, and prominent donor. The one thing that I was grateful for was that I never got that $15,000 from him. I would gladly leave that money and take my friend any day of the week. To this day, Cynthia and I have an even stronger bond because of that incident. And I have a better appreciation for what she lives with as a minority woman. Some people think that politics is nasty, and that campaigns are dirty and corrupt. Maybe that's true in some cases, but I tried really hard to conduct myself in a professional manner and lead my campaign with integrity. Don't get me wrong, politics can be a nasty game, but that particular individual wasn't involved in politics, he just tried to insert his beliefs into my political campaign. I wouldn't allow it, and I hope that you won't succumb to that kind of pressure either. There will always be people who attempt to influence your campaign, and once they make a donation, they believe that they are entitled to do so. But at the end of the day, it's your campaign, with your name on the signs and on the literature. It's up to you whether or not your campaign becomes nasty or corrupt. You get to draw the line and say what is acceptable and what is not. Set the standard early by surrounding yourself with trusted friends and highly ethical staff members, and you'll be able to look at yourself in the mirror at the end of your campaign, win or lose.

Finally, on a more positive note, no matter what, whether someone hosts an event for you or writes you a check for $5 or $5,000, show your gratitude and send a handwritten thank you note. I never sent emails or asked staff to write my thank you notes. Every Sunday afternoon, I sat myself down and wrote out personal thank you cards to every single person who donated to my campaign. Each week, my treasurer would give me a list of names and addresses of donors, and I would write them a personal note showing my heartfelt appreciation for their donation and support. Some people wrote back, saying how pleased they were to receive my note, because rarely do people send handwritten notes these days. And they would often include another check with that note! (Yes, I would send another thank you card.) You can ask Tom Winant, who got 13 thank you notes from me, one for every time he donated. Tom appreciated this simple gesture of appreciation so much that he gave more than just money. He spent many weekends walking door-to-door campaigning for me as well. Writing the thank you notes not only garnered continued support, it also gave me the opportunity once a week to look at a list of all of the people who believed in me and were investing in me. This ritual was a short respite from campaigning each and every week, a time when I could sit down and be really grateful—no matter what happened that week—there was this growing list of people who were out there cheering me on, and that kept me going for one more week.

Lesson 2: Know Your Numbers

The first question people will likely ask you about your campaign is, "How much money have you raised?" and the second question they'll likely ask is, "How many votes do you need to win?" You must know these answers off the top of your head and be able to say how you will get the necessary votes. In the campaign planning phase, the "exploratory" phase of decision making, go to the county elections office and ask for a file of the registered voters in your district. If you're running in a local election, you can request an electronic file of registered voters in that city. If your district crosses over into multiple counties, you may need visit each county elections office to get this information. Usually, the county will sell you a file with this information for a small fee. The electronic file will probably contain a list of registered voters, their party affiliation, whether they voted in the last election or last couple of elections, their address, and phone number. This spreadsheet can be helpful when you are making phone calls to voters asking for their support, or campaigning door-to-door. However, there is also free information available online from the elections department. You can find out how many people voted in the last election (voter turnout) and how many voted Republican, Democrat, or for a third-party candidate. You can also find out the total number of registered voters, as well as the total number of voters who are registered as Republicans and Democrats.

If you are running in a local, non-partisan race, the number of Republicans and Democrats may not matter, although you absolutely should not ignore this information just because the seat you're running for is non-partisan. A non-partisan race is one in which your name is on the ballot for a particular open seat, but there will not be a party affiliation next to your name. For example, most city and county council elections are non-partisan, as are elections for sheriffs, judges, and special districts like water or airport districts. When I ran for city council, the ballot listed my name as a candidate, but it did not have an "R" next to it, so arguably, voters did not know whether I was a Republican or Democrat at the time. However, in my experience, no political seat is non-partisan. While campaigning for a non-partisan city council seat, I was standing outside the grocery store introducing myself and handing out fliers to people as they went into the store. One woman asked my party affiliation and I said, "I'm a Republican, but this is a non-partisan election." She replied, "I could never vote for a Republican!" At this point, I should have just dropped it, but the critical thinking, analytical professor in me just couldn't let it go. I asked her why she wouldn't vote for a Republican even though this was a local, non-partisan election. She said it was because Republicans want to take away her right to choose an abortion. I assured her that not only was I pro-choice, but that the city council would not be making policy decisions about abortion—those would be left to the Supreme Court. It didn't matter, her mind was made up. I let the conversation drop, knowing that I wasn't going to change her mind there in front of the grocery store. Lesson learned: party affiliation does matter even in a non-partisan race! Be prepared for those types of discussions. And by the way, I also know several Republicans who have uttered the phrase, "I could never vote for a Democrat!", so the close-mindedness exists on both sides. Party affiliation is a powerful influence that sometimes defies logic. US President Richard Nixon still enjoyed over a 24% approval rating even as he faced impeachment!

You can get started pretty easily in small communities. When I was running for city council, we lived in a charming little town of about 15,000 residents. There were just over 5,000 registered voters, and I needed exactly 2,548 votes to win. One of the first things I did was to meet with the President of the Chamber of Commerce in order to share some of my pro-business positions. I also asked him for a list of local business owners, which he supplied. This gave me a solid start for garnering financial support, endorsements, and voter support.

Later, while running for Congress, it was a completely different ballgame. The district included territory in four counties with over 750,000 residents. There were 303,112 registered voters, and I needed exactly 151,557 votes to win. But the party affiliation breakdown was even more important than these numbers because I was running as a Republican in California, in a particularly liberal district. This breakdown didn't surprise me and probably won't surprise you, but what might surprise you is my naïve belief that I could overcome these odds. (Or maybe it was my scrappiness!)

Congressional District CA-20
Democrats: 54.2%
Republicans: 22.3%
DTS (decline to state): 16.8%

Yes, it's true, I thought that I could overcome these numbers. My logic went something like this: if I could get every single one of the Republicans and DTS voters to vote for me, that would give me 39.1%. Then I would persuade moderate Democrats to vote for me by targeting middle class voters who were parents, like me, or who wanted to see a woman represent this district for the first time ever. Yes, I knew that it would be a long shot and that it would be a tough challenge, but I was convinced it could be done. What I didn't take into account was the mysterious process called gerrymandering.

Let me demystify this long-established political strategy. Gerrymandering is the process of drawing state and national legislative districts in such a way as to benefit one party over the other. Imagine laying out a map and drawing lines around concentrations of voters who are favorable to your policy positions. As a result, we often see zig-zag patterns making up districts that have large groups of Republicans or Democrats, in an effort to reduce the number of competitive races. Steven Nass at Wikimedia depicts gerrymandering perfectly in the charts below.

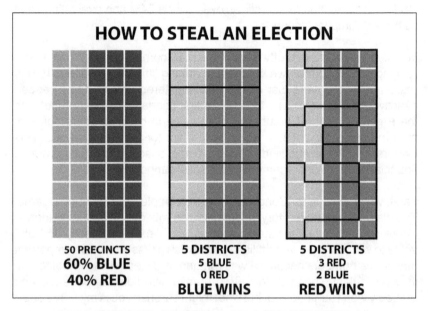

HOW TO STEAL AN ELECTION

50 PRECINCTS	5 DISTRICTS	5 DISTRICTS
60% BLUE	5 BLUE	3 RED
40% RED	0 RED	2 BLUE
	BLUE WINS	**RED WINS**

Image credit: Steven Nass, copyright 2/22/2015;
Creative Commons attribution, Share Alike 4.0 International.

The process of gerrymandering dates back to 1812 when the Governor of Massachusetts, whose name was Gerry, redrew the district boundaries in an attempt to benefit his Democratic-Republican party. Wait, what? Was that the Democratic party or the Republican party? That's right, from 1743 to 1826, critics of the Federalists banded together and formed the Republican party, but they were also known as the Democratic-Republican party. Back to Gerry—his gerrymandering didn't work out so well for him. In the 1812 election, the Massachusetts House and the governorship were lost to the Federalists and poor ol' Gerry lost his job. You would think that politicians would have given up on the idea of gerrymandering after that, but they didn't, and it still continues to this day. Gerrymandering, or redistricting, is usually done after a national census, and with a couple of objectives in mind: 1) spread voters of a particular type across several districts to deny them a large voting bloc in any one district, 2) concentrate many voters of one type into a single district to benefit one party, or 3) redraw two districts into one, thus forcing the two incumbents to run against each other, and eliminating one of them. These decisions are typically made by a non-partisan commissions nominated by the state governor. The legality of gerrymandering has been reviewed by the Supreme Court at least three times. Each time, the court found that redistricting, even when it benefits one political party, is not illegal or unconstitutional as long as it does not harm ethnic or racial minorities.

The maps below show some examples of redistricting that is intended to benefit one party. In the 22nd Congressional District of Texas, the map was redrawn in 2003 to move most of Fort Bend County into a different district, helping that district's Republican candidate, and placing most of Harris County and Galveston county in District 22, benefiting a Republican candidate there.

Similarly, Maryland's 3rd Congressional District, shown below, is made up of three oddly disjointed pieces, and the shape is so complex that it seems incomprehensible to even refer to it as a "district" in any sense except the political. It was redistricted several times in an effort to favor Democratic candidates. It has been called the most gerrymandered district in America. As a result, it's been a safe seat for Democrats for the past 90 years!

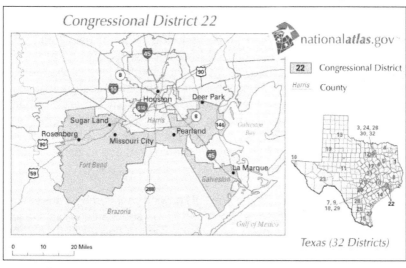

Texas's controversial 2003 partisan gerrymander produced TX District 22 for former Representative Tom DeLay, a Republican (image credit: nationalatlas.gov, public domain).

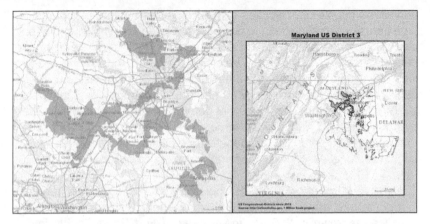

The New Republic has named Maryland's 3rd Congressional District as America's most gerrymandered district (image credit: nationalatlas.gov, public domain).

In CA-20, where I ran for Congress, the district has been redrawn or gerrymandered at least six times, in 1937, 1943, 1975, 1983, 1993, and 2013. From 1937 to 1976, the district bounced back and forth between Republicans and Democrats. Then in 1976, Leon Panetta was elected as a Democrat to CA-16, but it was subsequently redrawn to become CA-17, and later CA-20. From then on, it became a Democratic stronghold. As a result of gerrymandering, there are districts where Democrats are predetermined to win and others where Republicans are predetermined to win. Thanks to my idealism, I thought that voters actually had a say in who represented them, and that it wasn't just a game on a map. It seems ridiculous to me now, but I truly thought that I could change this reality and make our votes count. I strongly believed that as long as I knew the issues and could relate well to voters, party affiliation or party registration wouldn't be the deciding factor. Lesson learned! Fortunately, it's impossible to gerrymander by gender, so issues with broad and strong appeal to women or men can overcome these kinds of political map games.

This brings us back to the importance of knowing your numbers. It's critical that you know how many votes you need to win and the party registration percentages in your district. Dig in to the data to figure out if you can realistically get the necessary number of votes to win, especially given the way the district is drawn. Know the history of the district. Has that seat always been held by one party? If another party was ever successful, how many votes did they get and how much money did that candidate raise? If you determine that you can indeed achieve 50% +1 votes, then you need to find out where every single one of those people live and how you are going to reach them. Literally. The good news is, there's an app for that!

Technology is amazing and can be extremely helpful in a modern campaign. Gone are the days of printing lists of registered voters and precinct maps, and carrying clipboards door-to-door. Of course, like everything else in a political campaign, it costs money to buy accurate data and applications to effectively make use of that data. There are literally hundreds of companies that work with political campaigns to help them collect, compile, and analyze constituent information. My recommendation is to pay for this information in order to make the best use of your time. Don't cheap out, because you will waste time knocking on the wrong doors and calling the wrong voters.

You may have heard that President Obama used "big data" in the 2008 and 2012 campaigns, and that then-candidate Trump said that he was not using big data in his campaign in 2016. There have certainly been arguments on both sides about how useful this information can be. According to Chuck Todd and Carrie Dann, who studied and reported on big data in 2016, it's a "combination of massive technological power and endlessly detailed voter information—[which] has certainly changed the way campaigns are conducted. Like corporations, campaigns now know far more about their constituents than ever before—what they read, which movies they stream, which shows they watch, where they shop, which products they buy."[3]

You may wonder why that kind of information is even important. I can assure you that it's extremely useful because it can save your campaign a lot of time and money. For example, if you want to buy targeted advertising online or on TV, you can specifically place those ads during certain TV shows, or on specific websites, likely to be seen by your target voters. Thanks to big data, you'll know where to place your newspaper ads and what age group to target on Facebook. This approach is also known as "micro-targeting." Some argue that it can save candidates time and money, and help them get the votes they need to win. Others argue that it allows candidates to focus only on those who share a common position without having to convince dissenters. Eitan Hersh, who wrote *Hacking the Electorate,* says that if you have enough data about a person, you can predict how they will behave, and how they will vote.

---

[3]Sean Illing, "A Political Scientist Explains How Big Data is Transforming Politics," Vox, March 16, 2017.

Unfortunately, I had it all wrong in my campaign. I thought I just needed to get all of the Republicans and all of the DTS voters, and then convince *some* Democrats to vote for me, but this was completely backwards. The idea behind using big data, and behind any successful campaign, for that matter, is to identify your supporters and then convince them to go out and vote for you. My approach entailed finding people in the opposing party, convincing them to support me, and then persuading them to vote for me. Whew! No wonder I was exhausted! I was adding two extra steps that were nearly impossible to achieve. Thanks to big data analysis and election results, I now know that it's nearly impossible to change someone's mind—not only in politics, but in general.

Using data wisely can save your campaign a lot of time and energy, if it's part of a sound overall strategy. Admittedly, my strategy was neither sound nor logical. This is quite ironic because I have actually taught courses on strategy (not campaign strategy, obviously), and yet my own strategy fell short in so many ways. After mulling this over, I have come to the conclusion that my strong desire to serve, and my belief in the possibility of making a meaningful difference, blinded me to obstacles that now seem so obvious in retrospect. I thought voters had an appetite for someone new and different regardless of party affiliation. Clearly, there was an appetite for new and different (i.e., Trump), but I was wrong about the party affiliation part. That's okay, I chalk this up to a valuable life lesson and opportunity for personal growth (for those visual learners, please imagine the palm of my hand repeatedly hitting my forehead!). I don't mind openly revealing my flaws if my experiences help future candidates avoid these same mistakes. Many successful candidates write books about everything they did right, but rarely will they admit the things that they did wrong. Quite frankly, that doesn't help anyone. I've always learned more from my failures than from my successes, and I'd prefer to learn from other people's failures where possible.

While I'm admitting my shortcomings, I might as well add that I'm cheap too. There's no nice way to say it—I'm just miserly with money. As I've explained, I worked really hard to raise money for my campaign, so I was very protective of how we spent that money. I cheaped out on my website and on buying the data that could have really helped my campaign. Don't get me wrong, I don't think that a great website or an advanced app could have turned the tide on this particular election or changed the voter registration, but it certainly would have improved our overall campaign operations. The app we used was one that was purchased by the state Republican party, and we were given access to it for free since I was the Republican candidate in this race. However, the data in the app was outdated and, in many cases, inaccurate. Sometimes the app didn't work at all. For example, it was supposed to have a feature that allowed everyone involved to see which houses had already been contacted (either by a phone call or door knock), in order to avoid having multiple people from our campaign contact the same house. This feature didn't work, so my volunteers often crossed paths and duplicated efforts. Not to mention it's embarrassing when the homeowner says, "Yeah, someone already came here and told me all of this!" Bottom line: use a reputable company that gathers and compiles the most recent data, and supplies a 24/7 help desk for anyone using the application who needs help. It is worth the money, even if you're cheap like me!

You can also collect a lot of important information through your campaign website if you have a platform that allows you collect and organize data about who visits your website. When I ran for city council, I asked a friend to build my website and he did a great job. We purchased the domain name, caseylucius.com, and he built a static site that featured my pictures, my personal and professional background, and my positions on key issues. In a small, local campaign, this was all that was necessary, and it worked really well. However, if you are running in a state or national race, I highly recommend using a campaign-specific platform. You'll need a platform that can accommodate online donations, organize donors and volunteers, schedule and update events, track site traffic, maintain a supporter database, integrate social media, and allow for a current newsfeed.

Thrifty as I am, I tried to stay on budget, so I started out by asking a young college student to build my congressional campaign website. It looked fine when he was done, but the differences between this website and my council website was significant: 1) it would not be a static site, 2) we needed the ability to take online donations, and 3) we needed to collect voter information. In a competitive race, things are always changing, and you need to keep your website up to date. We posted media reports, endorsements, meet the candidate events, videos, pictures, and more on a weekly, and sometimes daily, basis. You definitely need a site that is easy to use and one that any member of your staff (including the candidate) can edit. At the beginning of my campaign, I wrote over 26 position papers on different issues, and our website had an "Issues" tab where people could see exactly where I stood on these issues. These included everything from abortion to gay marriage to desalination plants and ocean acidification. About halfway through the campaign, airplane noise and new flight routes became one of the hottest topics in the district. I had to quickly research the issue, write a position paper, put out a press release, and make a short video telling voters how seriously I believed this issue to be. We put all of that online and got it on social media, as well as to the print media, within a few days. We were only able to do that because I scrapped my original website and switched over to a campaign-specific platform.

We used a platform called "Campaign Partner" that cost only $50 per month, and it was worth every penny, primarily because it was so easy to update. Some of these platforms have a variety of monthly plans with different options. Depending on the size of your campaign and your budget, it's probably worth considering the biggest package available at the highest monthly rate. And this is the cheap lady talking! Trust me, you need to collect as much information on supporters as possible, and have it all organized in one convenient location. This will save you oodles of time and effort in dozens of ways. For example, when you are looking for supporters to put up yard signs, you'll already have a handy database of people with yards that includes their names and addresses. It sounds simple, and choosing the right campaign information system makes sure that it is.

You'll also need to use your website to collect voter data. Each time someone visits your campaign website, they should be encouraged (maybe even forced) to enter their name and email address. This helps build that ever-so-important contact list that you'll email updates to periodically. If someone happened to check out your website out of curiosity, hopefully, you'll win over their support after a couple of persuasive email updates. If someone donates online, it's even better, because you can set up the page to require that they fill out a form with their name, address, email, phone number, and occupation. You can then use that information for yard sign information, endorsements, and consider seeking out others in their industry who might share their concerns in order to get their support. Truly, the more information you can collect, the better. You can even add a short survey to the website to get voters' views on particular issues. The objective here is to better understand the voters so you'll know how to engage them.

Unlike investment performance, past voter behavior is the greatest predictor of future voting behavior. This means that you don't really have to spend time or money persuading people to vote for you, or trying to push your positions on any particular issues. You just need to find the people who are most likely to vote for you based on their past voting record and voter registration, and then get them to show up and actually vote for you. What does it mean to get them to show up and vote for you?

It's all about how you can mobilize voters. According to the Center for Information and Research on Civic Learning and Engagement (CIRCLE), the most effective way to engage a voter is an in-person door knock. When you get to that door, the most useful approach is to draw distinctions between the two candidates. This works best to mobilize voters, in part because voters see this comparison as the most truthful approach.[4] As you have probably experienced, the least effective way is an automated phone call. Personalizing voter engagement helps increase voter turnout. Even simply telling a voter where to vote and when to vote without explicitly asking them to vote for you is deemed helpful and likely to increase voter turnout in your favor.

There is some interesting research about the impact of younger voters, and why getting out their vote can have compounded benefits. It turns out there's a "trickle up" effect whereby younger voters activate older adults living in the same household. So, it's not only important to know your numbers when it comes to voter registration, but it's just as important to know the age of the voters. You'll also need to know voting history, education, and vote by mail (so-called "absentee voting") history within households, and then use that information to target those younger voters.

A final point about knowing your numbers and your voters is to know how many people vote by mail. If your state is one of the early voting states and allows vote by mail ballots, you may actually have to spend additional money to target voters twice—once when the ballots are mailed out, and again right before election day for those who will vote at the polls. Absentee voting actually has the effect of moving the election date up and shortening the time candidates have for their get-out-the-vote efforts. In 2008, a surprising 42% of California voters voted by mail. I was one of them. Let's face it, it's more convenient to vote from your kitchen table rather than stand in a line on election day. And it gives you more time to read through the ballot, some of which can be an intimidating 30 pages long, including propositions, for and against arguments, as well as the candidate statements.

If you know who will vote by mail, then your campaign can concentrate on those voters well before the ballots are mailed out, which is usually about three weeks before the election. The county elections department can provide a list of absentee voters, as well as a list of ballots that have been mailed. You can even keep track of who has and who hasn't voted

---

[4]Kathleen Hall Jamieson, *Everything You Think You Know About Politics, and Why You're Wrong* (New York: Basic Books, 2000), 107-110.

in the current election. I thought this was kind of creepy, but if you have the staff and resources to do it, don't hesitate to call those voters and remind them to mail in their ballots, especially if they are your supporters.

Let me wrap up this chapter with a short story about why it's so important to know your numbers. When I began my race for Congress, I had coffee with a prominent Republican party member. He held a seat on the county Republican Central Committee, and was influential in the state and national Republican party. I shared my intention to run and asked for his support. Because I hadn't entered the race yet, he didn't ask about money, but he did ask how many votes I needed to win. I told him 151,557. He then asked about the breakdown of party affiliation, and I gave him those numbers. He asked me how I planned on reaching 151,557 voters, most of whom were Democrats. He also asked me where they lived, their gender, and their ages. I didn't have any of this information yet! He advised me to have a plan, not just a campaign plan or a fundraising plan, but a plan to meaningfully engage those 151,557 voters. He told me that no one would support me unless I could demonstrate how I could reasonably expect to get 151,557 votes. I left that coffee meeting feeling pretty discouraged and a little pissed off! As I reviewed our meeting in my head, I kept thinking, "Hey, this guy is in the Republican leadership, and I'm a Republican wanting to make a sacrifice and run for office, so he should be thanking me, not quizzing me!" But he was right. And he wasn't the last person to ask me those questions. Even if you're a Republican in a Republican district, or a Democrat in a Democratic district, don't assume that you can get the votes you need to win. You have to gather the data, know where every single one of those voters live, and have a plan to stalk them for the next 12 months! Just kidding, stalking is illegal. But you do need a plan to engage them multiple times, motivate them, and mobilize them to vote for you. Without this information and a well-thought-out plan, none of the other stuff matters. It doesn't matter how cute your family is, or how long you served in the military, or how many volunteer activities you've done, or how smart you are on the issues. Party leaders won't be impressed by that. You have to be able to reach the voters you need to win, and that means collecting the data and raising the money to target them.

My grandma used to say, "Getting old isn't for sissies." Neither is campaigning!

Lesson 3: Your Political Party May Not Support You

This one might not surprise you, but it sure surprised me! I assumed that, because I was a Republican running in a partisan race, with an R next to my name on the ballot, that the Republican party would support me and Republicans would vote for me. Oh boy, was I wrong!

Remember the story about the prominent Republican who asked me all the questions about numbers of voters? Well, not only did he not support my candidacy, but he actually supported my Democratic opponent! He said it was because they were longtime friends. Nevertheless, he was in a leadership role in the county Republican party, as well as the state party. These are the kind of things that I was just completely unprepared for, but hopefully, you will be prepared after reading this book.

When I was in third grade, I asked my mom if we were Republicans or Democrats. The conversation went something like this:

Me: Mom, are we Republicans or Democrats?

Mom: We're Democrats.

Me: Why?

Mom: Because Democrats support the working class and we're working class.

Me: Okay. (But in truth, it really wasn't okay, because I was wondering why we'd want to be part of a group that would keep us in the working class. I mean, wouldn't we want to get out of the working class and into some other class?)

Fast forward to my time in college at Ashland University in Ohio, studying political science. I was an Ashbrook Scholar, which was a program named after John Ashbrook, a former Republican Senator. The program reinforced the basic ideas of the Founders of the United States, and required that we study the Federalist papers and the US Constitution.

I also began studying the principles of the two main parties. It turns out that my mom was right, the Democratic party does believe in greater equality for all, including among those of differing incomes. They are also committed to ensuring that the same opportunities are available to people regardless of class, gender, or ethnicity. But where I think my mom was wrong was in the Party's role. She thought that someone, somewhere, was advocating for her, helping her. She thought that Democrats and their policies would somehow elevate her position and her standard of living. Unfortunately, that never happened. My mom always worked hard, and still lived paycheck-to-paycheck long after I left home. There was no person, policy, or party that offered her more. I began to wonder if what the working-class people like my family were seeking was economic stability rather than economic growth. Even though I was told at a young age that I was a Democrat, and that we were working class, I struggled with this. I didn't want that same life. It may not be accurate, but I associated Democrat with blue-collar jobs, and I didn't want to be a blue-collar worker. So, when I registered to vote for the first time, I registered as a Republican. Sorry, Mom!

No, I'm not trying to convince anyone to become a Republican. In fact, after this chapter, you may want to run far away from the Republican party and possibly from all political parties. Personally, I had a higher expectation of the Republican party. Just like my mom believed that her party was advocating for her, I assumed that my party was working on my behalf. I was convinced that Republicans also believed in opportunity and equality, and I was inspired by the fact that the first women to hold seats in the House and the Senate were Republican. It was a Republican who issued the Emancipation Proclamation, and it was a Republican-controlled Congress that passed the 13th Amendment abolishing slavery. What's more, the first African-American governor was a Republican, and it was a Republican-controlled Congress that passed the 19th Amendment guaranteeing women the right to vote. And there's more! The first Hispanic Senator and the first Asian-American Senator were both Republicans. Supreme Court Justice Earl Warren, a former Republican, struck down racial segregation in public schools. I was proud of these accomplishments by Republicans, and this is the kind of upward mobility and opportunity that inspired me to register as a Republican. Plus, my mom said, "Republicans are all rich." That cinched the deal for me. If that was true, then I definitely wanted to be a Republican!

When my husband and I first moved to California in 2008, I got involved in the county Republican party. I was new to the area and didn't know anyone, so one of the first things I did was join the Monterey Bay

Republican Women Federation. (There is also a Democratic Women's Federation with clubs in nearly every city.) I volunteered for a short time before being asked to be president of the club. It sounds flattering, but the club was made up of mostly older ladies, and I think most of them were just too tired to take on the task. They saw me as a new and eager young lady, and jumped at the opportunity to toss this leadership role my way. It turns out that I really enjoyed it. I was the club president for one year, until I had my son, and had to take a break from lunching with the ladies. Also, in 2008, I volunteered on the McCain for President campaign. I felt a certain personal affinity to John McCain because my husband and I had lived in Hanoi, Vietnam, for three years, and the apartment we lived in was just across the street from the lake where John McCain had been shot down. In 1967, then-Lieutenant McCain was flying an A-4 jet over North Vietnam during the US-Vietnam War, when his airplane was shot down. He and the plane landed in a lake in the center of Hanoi. He was pulled out of the lake by some local farmers, beaten, and dragged off to prison where he remained for the next seven years. To this day, there is a small stone monument near that lake acknowledging the heroes who captured the enemy, John McCain. I saw that monument almost every day for three years, and had great respect for both his service in the military, and for what he endured in a Vietnamese prison. Thus, I volunteered to work on his presidential campaign.

Monterey County had set up a small campaign office. That's where I worked, raised money, handed out yard signs, and met lots of people who were also interested in supporting McCain. One nice thing about this experience was that I got to meet everyone associated with the local Republican party. Between this campaign and the women's club, I created a pretty robust network among local Republicans.

In 2010, a woman who was the former mayor of Pacific Grove was running for the regional water district and asked me to volunteer on her campaign. I really liked her and believed in what she wanted to accomplish, so I gladly helped out. This was much different than my experience with the McCain campaign because this was a real grassroots effort. We had staff meetings once each week, met with her campaign manager, devised a media and advertising strategy, mobilized college Republicans to walk door-to-door, spent time making phone calls, and more. It was a terrific opportunity to experience the real nuts and bolts of campaigning at the local level. I went through every detail of the process with her, everything from ordering remittance envelopes, to building a website, picking colors and fonts for yard signs, designing a tri-fold flier, and debate preparations. If there's one thing that helped prepare me for my own campaigns, it was working on Jeanne Byrne's campaign for the water district. I got to see how she solicited endorsements from the realtors' association and the hospitality association. I witnessed firsthand how her finance committee made lists of donors and nagged those donors relentlessly until they gave money. I even became good friends with her treasurer and campaign consultant, who would later help me with my campaigns. If you are thinking about running for office, first consider working on someone else's campaign, especially at the local level. Working on a big state or national campaign might draw greater attention, but I guarantee you will learn a whole lot more if you work on a local or county campaign.

When I ran for city council in 2012, I had Jeanne's campaign model to guide me. I knew who donated to her campaign, who endorsed her, which media outlets could be trusted, who to avoid, and even where to order my thank you cards. Details like thank you cards may sound silly, but when you're starting a campaign, there is so much that you don't know. Every bit of experience helps! Even figuring out what paperwork you have to file with the city clerk or the secretary of state can be very overwhelming at first. Having someone who has been through a campaign who can tell you where to order yard signs and how many to order, what should be printed on your remittance envelopes, and introduce you to the local press, can be extremely helpful and save you a lot of time and aggravation.

When I ran for city council in 2012, it was a non-partisan race, but because I had developed friends and contacts in the local Republican party, they eagerly supported my race. Mostly, they were excited to see a younger woman run for office, and they knew that my military background and having earned a PhD would make me a strong candidate. There were no controversial issues at the local level to create any concern for my base supporters. The ladies from the Women's Republican Club helped by stuffing envelopes and making phone calls to donors. I employed (with pizza) the college Republicans to walk door-to-door, and many local Republicans donated to my race. The Republican party even sent out a mailer with my name and photo on it, encouraging voters in Pacific Grove to vote "Casey for Council."

I have to admit, though, that the real ticket to success in my city council race was not a result of the efforts of the Republican party, or even my own efforts. It was the firefighters who saved the day. I had been interviewed by the firefighters' association (the IAFF), and they decided to endorse me. I grew to love these firefighters because they didn't just give me their endorsement, they paid for a mailer and walked door-to-door distributing my flier, all the while wearing their IAFF t-shirts. Come on, everyone loves it when a firefighter shows up at their door, right? The next best thing would have been to have a Casey for Council calendar with pictures of firefighters . . . but I digress.

I wish that my race for the US Congress would have been as light-hearted and easy as my race for city council. It wasn't. I struggled with the Republican party from day one. My problems started with the prominent Republican coffee meeting that made me want to stop drinking coffee, and the challenges continued throughout the entire campaign. As I said at the beginning of this chapter, it really surprised me that my own party wouldn't be eager to support me in this race. Looking back, I somewhat see their perspective. They must have been thinking, "Why should we spend money on someone who can't win, when we could instead spend our money on Republicans who can win?" This is a sound argument, but the fact was that those other Republicans were running in non-partisan races, and didn't have a "R" next to their name on the ballot. I was the one sticking my neck out there in a partisan race, in a Democratic district, no less, trying to make the case that a Republican could win. It sure didn't help when even Republicans were saying that I couldn't win!

I remember one of the first meetings that I had with the chair of the county Republican party. I asked him for donor lists, and he refused. He also had a favorite campaign manager that he wanted me to use, but that particular person had a very bad reputation as being unethical and generally kind of sleazy. I knew this, and I never really liked the guy anyway, so I told the chair that I had no plans to use that campaign manager. He told me in so many words that if I didn't run my campaign his way, then he would make it difficult for me. Well, all you have to do is tell a scrappy lady that she has to do things "your way," and you're pretty much guaranteed that's not going to happen! Unfortunately, my defiance hurt me in the long run. The chair of the party was very influential because he had raised a lot of money, he knew donors, and many people called him to ask his advice on which candidate to support. After I denied his request to hire the seedy campaign manager, he used every opportunity to undermine my candidacy. I know this because some of my donors told me that they had talked to him, and he had told them not to donate to my campaign. Can you imagine, your own party working against you? Hmmm, I'm guessing Bernie Sanders knows exactly how that feels. That's right, regrettably, this sort of thing happens at all levels and within both parties.

I decided at that point to bypass the local party and talk directly to our state party leadership. There, I was told that the state Republican party was not interested in my race because they were focusing on those candidates running for the state legislature. Okay, that makes sense. But then they also told me that the Republican party's strategy in California was to support candidates in non-partisan races. I didn't get this logic at all. Why support those in races who don't have to affiliate with a party? It turns out that the answer is, basically, because it's easier. It's easier in some states to get certain candidates elected as judges, sheriffs, council members, and county supervisors than it is to get candidates elected into higher level positions in seats that are dominated by the opposite party. I get that it's easier, but I've never been one to take the easy way, so to me, this is just plain irritating! This was one kind of party that definitely was NOT fun!

About six months into my 17-month campaign, I was tempted to leave party politics behind, and change my voter registration party affiliation to Independent, and run for Congress as an Independent candidate. I wasn't sure how this would go over with Republican voters, or Democrats, for that matter, but I was fed up. Then I met Kip Hawley. He was a local resident who had watched me during my tenure on the city council, had been tracking my campaign, and was interested in helping me. He had also worked in the Reagan Administration, the George H.W. Bush Administration, and the George W. Bush Administration. I told him everything that was going on with the local party (and more to the point, without the party), and he told me to go straight to Washington, DC, and appeal to the National Republican party, specifically, the National Republican Congressional Committee (NRCC). He also advised me to hire a national campaign consultant and a proper campaign staff. He walked into my life just at the right time, shook up my campaign operations in a way that we needed to be shaken up, and believed in me when I was greatly in need of encouragement.

Onward to Washington, DC! In the winter of 2016, I flew to Washington, DC, to introduce myself to the NRCC leadership and to my new campaign consultant. It was a very encouraging visit because I learned about the Young Guns program, in which national Republican candidates meet certain milestones that enable them to advance through this program and ultimately earn the endorsement of the Speaker of the House, as well as earn the financial support of the Republican party. The first step was to raise $100,000 to earn the right to be considered "On the Radar." The second step was a secret! It was a target amount of money, but it wasn't clear what the amount was. I was guessing that perhaps $400,000 or more would get me "Contender" status, but I had no idea what was required to get to the final stage, which was being declared a "Young Gun." Oh, and I don't know why this term was chosen—seems like there are perhaps a million more appealing possibilities that wouldn't exclude older people, and wouldn't refer to a weapon, but that's just me.

Filled with renewed hope, I flew back to California and commenced intense fundraising to meet that $100,000 goal. As a "reward," the NRCC sent me a password-protected website where about 30 issues relevant to the election were listed along with arguments and counter-arguments for each of those issues. This was intended to help candidates develop their campaign platform and practice for debates. Since I had already been campaigning for seven months, I already had established my platform and I had already participated in several debates. I also had various policy positions on my website, which I had written myself based on thorough research of that topic and the needs of my district. I had no interest in simply regurgitating the Republican position on issues such as immigration, for example, when immigration was such an important topic in my agricultural district, and required a specific and thoughtful response. The second thing that the NRCC sent me after being placed "On the Radar" was a packet of information that I needed to fill out and send back to them. This packet was a hefty 57 pages, and here's some of what was required:

- Finance goals
- Voter contact plan
- Absentee voters outreach plan
- Media training
- Plan to "track" opponent
- Budget
- Campaign staff with bios
- Digital campaign plan
- Voter tracking

Everything listed here is very important and necessary for any campaign planning, especially a national campaign, but much of this list referred to areas where I needed help from the national party. Instead, they were asking me to provide the answers. For example, I didn't even know what it meant to "track" my opponent (it basically means to hire someone to follow your opponent around and catch them saying something stupid on audio or video.) Once I found out what tracking meant, I had less than zero interest in spending my resources that way. Yes, I had financial goals, but I needed the party's help in reaching those goals. And I had a voter contact plan, but my small staff wouldn't be enough to implement that plan in addition to doing everything else that needed to be done. This would have been a helpful packet of information to receive back when

I was in the planning and exploratory phases of the campaign, perhaps when I had my first coffee meeting with that prominent Republican. Instead of asking all those questions, he could have handed me this 57-page packet with the admonition to develop this plan and demonstrate how I would implement it in exchange for the party's support. But instead, it appeared to me at that time that this document was held back as some kind of secret. Only those candidates who have raised $100,000 are worthy to see this packet. Why? And why did I have to jump through hoops to get my own party to get behind me? Sheesh!

Ultimately, I did fill out this massive form and answer all of the questions, even the ones that said, "Has the candidate's wife ever been arrested?" I had to laugh out loud at this one. It still says, "candidate's wife"! There is still the assumption that all of the candidates are men! Clearly, this document hasn't been updated since the last century. If anyone from the NRCC is reading this, could you please have someone replace each "wife" with "spouse or partner" in these documents? My relationship with the NRCC was short-lived because I never made it to Contender status. Maybe I would have qualified for this status, because I did raise over $400,000, but I didn't pursue it. I was too busy campaigning to beg them to help me. Although maybe I should have, because I never got a penny from anyone in the Republican leadership. I didn't get the Speaker's endorsement, and I didn't become a Young Gun. Maybe I could have been successful without these things, but it might have helped balance out the fight, especially when my opponent had opportunities like having Hillary Clinton come to town and being called up on stage to introduce her. How could I compete with that?

I have to admit, it wasn't all bad news when it came to interacting with the Republican party. I had some pretty cool things happen during my campaign. I got to meet Paul Ryan and Bret Baier. Just as I was surprised by the people who didn't support me, I was also pleasantly surprised by the people who did. There was one man I hadn't met, Dr. Charlie Kupperman, who had worked in the Reagan Administration, and he connected me with Paul Ryan's staff. When Speaker Ryan came to San Francisco for a fundraiser, I was invited by the staff to attend. We talked about my race, and he was very gracious. No matter what your politics, I can tell you that it's pretty cool to meet the Speaker of the House, third in line to the Presidency.

Image: Speaker of the House Paul Ryan with Casey, June 28, 2016

About the same time, Bill Warner, my pseudo-bundler, hosted Bret Baier at Pebble Beach for a golf tournament. He invited me to come to the golf club afterward to meet Bret and tell him about the race. This gave me a chance to make my case and try to get some national press coverage. It worked! He was interested in the race partly because Leon Panetta's son was my opponent, but also because it was an open seat and had never been held by a woman. It hadn't been won by a Republican in 40 years, so he thought viewers might be excited to get behind my campaign. As a result, a few months later, I was interviewed by Fox News, and *Special Report with Bret Baier* did a segment about our CA-20 Congressional race. I also had the chance to do a national radio interview with David Webb on Sirius XM radio about national security and the 2016 Orlando nightclub shooting. So, it wouldn't be fair to say that Republicans weren't supporting me, it's just that the party apparatus wasn't at all helpful. Of course, they may have been a bit distracted with their 2016 presidential candidate!

Considering the role that your political party will play in your campaign is extremely important. Before your race begins, think about whether or not your party's endorsement is important to you. Do you need their help with fundraising or coordinating volunteers? Do you want to be affiliated with a particular party and its platform? These are all important things to think about before you get started. If you decide you do want their support, develop a plan for securing the support that you need.

If you plan to run in a non-partisan race, like city council or judge, perhaps getting your party's backing is not necessary. However, if you are running for a State or National seat, you will have to deal with these questions of political party support whether you want to or not. If you want to avoid the political party drama, you could register as an Independent and present yourself as an independent thinker and political outsider. This will appeal to many voters, especially all the registered Independents. However, you'll need to figure out how to win the support of Republican and Democratic voters. Why should they vote for an Independent when they could vote for someone in their own party?

If you decide to move forward with your campaign as a Republican or Democratic candidate, engage your party early. Make appointments with local and state party leadership. Ask them what their expectations are of you. Ask them up front if they have certain staff or management team members that you should use. Even if you don't want to use their folks, don't refuse outright. Instead, offer to interview those individuals and let them know that you will keep an open mind about including them on your campaign team. If they insist that you use a particular campaign manager or staffer, ask if the party will pay that person's salary. I'm serious! If they want you to hire someone, they should be willing to foot the bill, or at least part of the bill.

During these initial meetings, ask if the party has office space you can use or phones for phone banking. Can you use their copier or printers? Find out if they already have a group of volunteers and a volunteer coordinator. If you are going to run as a representative of this party, you need to get the most out of your partnership, as well as maximize their contributions to your campaign. Be sure to ask how you can secure your party's endorsement early. Sometimes, if there is more than one Republican or Democrat running in the primary, the party will not endorse anyone until after the primary. I don't quite understand this because, by the time the primary is over, the campaign is pretty far along, and much of the fundraising and staffing is already underway, that the endorsement is not very useful. Get their endorsement sooner rather than later so that you can leverage that endorsement to raise money and build support for your candidacy among key individuals. If they insist on waiting until after the primary, suggest that the party host a debate between the internal candidates and then let the party leadership decide who to support following that debate. Be proactive with them and encourage them to be proactive in your race.

It's important to start seeking support at the local level before jumping to the state and national level. Once you secure local party support, you can confidently go to the state party leadership and solicit their support. By then, you should have a few prominent people backing you, which will make it much more convincing when you show up in Washington, DC and start asking for endorsements from national officials and the national party. Don't assume that you'll get support at any of these levels! Usually, the party is juggling a dozen local races, maybe 50 or 100 state races, and they have several hundred candidates bugging them for support at the national level. You are only one of these hundreds of candidates, and you really do have to be patient. But keep being scrappy, too! Don't accept "no" for an answer. You need to stick to your guns even after you have been rejected multiple times. Being scrappy means seeing every rejection as another step closer to success!

You also need to be patient and persistent with the party leadership because you'll likely need their help with fundraising. It can be difficult to find donors, but these individuals know donors, and they talk to a lot of people every day who could end up donating to your campaign. You need them saying great things about you, even if they're saying, "This is a tough race and she's got an uphill battle, but I know if she has our support, she can win." It doesn't have to be a rosy message about how great you are, as long as they're getting voters and donors behind you. That's what matters.

Pundits often say, "secure your base." I've never really understood this because I assumed that, if I was a Republican running for office, Republicans would vote for me. Shouldn't I spend my time talking to Democrats and Independents to earn their support? The short answer is, no. Spend time making people in your own party happy. These are the people who will walk door-to-door for you. They'll host events for you, and show up to cheer you on at other events. These are the people who will donate to you and tell their neighbors about you. There was one very active Republican volunteer who was always working in the local party office. She knew me very well and I thought she liked me. We disagreed on some issues. I was more moderate and she was more conservative.

I heard from a friend that, during my Congressional campaign, this woman told everyone at a large dinner party that I could never win, and furthermore that I shouldn't win, because I was too liberal! Geez, who needs an opposition party when you've got people like this in your own party? It was very disappointing, but I realized that my shortcoming boiled down to not securing my base. I needed to woo them to earn their support, rather than just assume that they would help me because we were in the same party.

Finally, let me share a few other organizations outside of the political parties that might help with your campaign. In California, I attended a one-year program called "Leadership Monterey." These types of leadership programs are offered in almost every city, and they are usually run by the Chamber of Commerce or a non-profit. They're educational programs that introduce the participants to different sectors and issues in the region. For example, we spent one day visiting farms and talking about water, immigration, labor, and all things agriculture. We spent another day visiting a local TV station and newspaper company, learning about the media process. After one year, I knew much more about the region where I lived, and I met some fabulous people! The other participants in my class became life-long friends, and I created a network of contacts in nearly every business sector in the county. This was extremely helpful when I first ran for office in 2012. I knew who to contact at the local newspaper because I had personally met that person through Leadership Monterey. I knew who to contact at the Realtors Association to ask for their endorsement because I had also met that person during the program. I would highly recommend getting involved in your local leadership program before you run for office so that you can better understand the issues, as well as make some important connections.

I also became a member of a non-partisan organization called California Women Lead. Again, these types of organizations exist in nearly every state, and they are a terrific way to meet other women who are interested in running for office, but don't want to get bogged down in party politics. These organizations host conferences focused on empowering women and training women to run for public office. These events provide access to like-minded individuals and will enable you to create a great network of support from all over the state. They also help women apply for positions on county and state boards and commissions. As I mentioned, I was on the local Traffic Safety Commission, a position appointed by the mayor. But there are also state commissions, like the Small Business Board or the Student Aid Commission, and these are appointed by the governor. Being on a state board or commission is a great entry point for running for office because you'll gain insight into the political process, experience working with a diverse board, and get connected to elected officials who can be of great help when you decide to run for office.

Another program that I found quite valuable was the Bergeson Series, a five-month program to train women to run for office in California. The program was named after Marian Bergeson, the first woman ever to serve in both the California State Assembly and the State Senate. She also was later appointed to be the State Secretary of Education. This program included media and fundraising training, and generally taught us the basics of how to run a campaign. There are similar organizations across the US. I found this experience to be very helpful and encouraging. One of the exercises we did in this program was to practice calling a donor, a local business owner, to ask for a donation. It was a real phone call with a real person on the other end of the phone. I made the call, introduced myself, and asked for a donation to support my hypothetical campaign. This was great practice, and if you have never done something like this, I highly recommend it!

Organizations like this are aimed specifically at women, but there are many organizations that serve both men and women, connecting them to elected officials, training potential candidates, and walking them through the process of running for office. Start with a basic internet search of organizations in your county or state, get involved, and start building your network! These organizations are a welcome departure from business-as-usual party politics. I don't think you can completely avoid the political parties, but you can certainly supplement your network and experiences with these types of organizations and their members.

Lesson 4: Your Family and Friends May Not Support You

In 2010, long before I ran for city council or Congress, I attended a four-week campaign school. This was extremely helpful, and I would definitely recommend looking around your city or county to see if such a program is offered. I think I paid $40 for four classes, and it included dinner, since the classes were held in the evenings. I love these types of events because I'm very social and I like to meet new people. And I love any event where food is offered! I also like to learn new things, and since I thought I might be running for office someday, I figured there was much to learn. Each week focused on a different theme, from writing a campaign plan to messaging to raising money. When it came to raising money, one of the recommendations was to make a list of 100 people that you could call to ask for a donation. I remember that someone drew a diagram on the whiteboard that was a circle with a smaller circle inside. She said when you start raising money, you start with your inner circle—your family and friends. Your inner circle should make up the bulk of the list of 100 contacts. Then you move to your outer circle made of people you know at work, church, your child's school, or people from other organizations. These are people you know, but not well enough to call them out of the blue and ask for money. I also remember she said that if you can't think of 100 people to call, you shouldn't run for office! Yikes, that's intimidating.

In case you haven't done this, it's a good exercise. It's extremely difficult to think of 100 people that you want to call and ask for money. Think of people who know you and know your heart. My list started with parents, siblings, aunts, uncles, cousins, grandparents, and in-laws, then I still had about 75 names to go, so I started adding friends from high school and college, neighbors who I talked to regularly, and coworkers who I talked to everyday. I think this got me about 50 more names. Twenty-five to go. Then I pulled out my Christmas card list. There were people who I didn't talk to every day, but I liked them well enough to send them a card every year, so I added them to my list. I made it to 100. Then the hard work begins—you have to start calling. I started with the easy ones first: family members.

I'm the first to admit that I made mistakes in my campaign, but probably the biggest mistake was assuming that certain people would support me. Just like I thought the Republican party would eagerly help with my campaign, I believed my best friends and family members would do the same. Imagine that you receive a cancer diagnosis, and you call your family and closest friends to tell them the bad news. They would probably all come running to help you in any way they could, right? They'd cook meals, help you with the kids, contribute financially to your medical bills, and provide the moral support required to get you through that challenging time. Now, imagine you announce to these same friends and family that you want to run for office . . . and there is silence. No one comes running, no one cooks meals or helps with the kids, and no one offers financial support. That's okay. After all, you don't have cancer. This is probably a bad analogy because running for office is not like having cancer, but it does convey the emotional intensity of my disappointment with the lack of support that I encountered. When you're facing a big challenge in life, naturally, you want your family to support you. While I was unpleasantly surprised when this support wasn't forthcoming, I decided to just wait and let the news settle in and then circle back after a few weeks. Weeks went by, but still nothing. As it turns out, and as most of you probably already know, politics is so divisive it can create tension even among family members. While you may think that the people you love will be excited for you, in fact, they may not want to have anything to do with you or your campaign. This can be both surprising and heartbreaking.

As I've mentioned, my step-dad, Ernie, worked in a factory and cashed in part of his retirement to help me pay for college. Ernie and my mom were my biggest fans. They cheered me on in high school, in college, and when I joined the US Navy. Ernie even drove me across the country when the Navy stationed me in San Diego, carting all of my worldly belongings from Virginia Beach. He also flew to Vietnam to visit me when we were living and working in Hanoi. Ernie was 100% on "Team Casey." When he died in 2013, I lost one of my biggest fans. My mom always picked up the slack, though, and she has more than filled in as my cheerleader and encourager. Then there's my biological father. I didn't grow up with my dad because he lived in Florida and I was raised in Ohio. Nevertheless, we've always had a good relationship. My dad owned a thriving homebuilding business, and was able to retire early as a result of his financial success. I have to admit, I was always a bit jealous as a kid because my sister and I grew up in an apartment living paycheck-to-paycheck while my brothers lived an entirely different, and more luxurious, existence with my dad and step-mom. When I started my campaign, I announced my candidacy to my dad, and he was very excited for me. I asked for a donation and his response was that he would pray about it. I'm fine with prayer, but sometimes I think this is used as a delaying tactic so people don't have to confront a difficult situation.

After a few weeks, I contacted my dad again to ask if he would donate to my campaign. I knew my dad and step-mom could afford to make a maximum donation, and they could possibly even write me a check for $10,800 to cover both the primary and general elections. Now, up until this time, I had never asked my dad for money, or for anything really, so I thought that he would be eager to support me financially this time. I honestly expected their full support, and thought he'd eventually make a contribution. Upon my second request, I got the same answer—that he had to pray about it. That's okay, if I was going to write a big, fat check to someone, I might pray about it, too!

A couple of weeks later, I received a four-page letter in the mail from my dad and step-mom explaining why they could not support my campaign. They had read through my website and found that my positions on certain issues did not align with their values. In fact, they found them to be "unprincipled." I'm not convinced that they read all of my policy positions, but they definitely read the two that mattered to them: marriage equality and abortion. My dad and his wife were disappointed to find that I believe in both the right to choose an abortion and the right to marriage between consenting adults. Their lengthy letter quoted scripture, and basically said that they could not support me because I was not following Biblical principles. I was heartbroken, not because I wasn't getting a hefty donation from my dad, but because my dad had concluded that I was an immoral person, or at very least, an immoral candidate, because of my position on these two issues.

Sure, a donation of $10,800 would have been nice, but what would have really made my day would have been a check for $100 with a note that said, "We're proud of you." All it takes to lift up any candidate, or any person, for that matter, is a sincere note of appreciation and a token of support. I'm pleased to share that I did receive such notes and checks from my siblings and other family members. I have since communicated with my dad about this, and let him know that I didn't think it was fair to be judged on these two issues. There are so many other accomplishments in my life, and a multitude of other positions that I have taken, that I could be judged on. Why only these two issues? It didn't matter what else I stood for or against. For my dad, these two issues were deal breakers, as they are with many conservative voters. That's the way it is in politics. Each voter and every single donor gets to decide what they like or don't like about the candidate and their positions. This reality doesn't change just because someone is a family member, it just makes it a little harder to accept.

Similarly, I had dinner with one of my best friends, and over dinner, she grilled me on the issue of abortion. I talked to her honestly about how I struggled with this issue. For a long time, I was staunchly pro-life, but a friend of mine was faced with the difficult decision of whether or not to continue a pregnancy knowing that her baby was severely disabled. At that point, I concluded that only she and her husband should be able to make that difficult and heartbreaking decision. I'm convinced that the government shouldn't tell her what she *has* to do in such a complex and personal situation. I know it's a contentious issue. I know it's a divisive issue. I explained my position honestly to my friend, but I also felt annoyed that I had to sit through dinner and have this conversation at all. Couldn't she support me, in spite of our differences on this issue, just because we're friends? Later, I realized that one of the reasons she's my friend is because she's a strong woman and an independent thinker, and she always challenges me to be a better person. If she didn't ask me these questions, I would have respected her less. You can imagine that I was blown away a few days later, when I received a very generous donation from her and her husband. This is true friendship, when you can disagree on an issue but still hear each other out and respect one another's opinion. She was there for me when I needed her, even though it wasn't cancer, it was just a campaign.

I had other extended family members send me notes or emails explaining they couldn't financially support my campaign. If you are considering donating to a friend or relative who is a candidate and you're feeling hesitant, please just don't send the check. Based on my experience, you're better off sparing them the note saying why you're not contributing. Or, if you want to preserve your relationships, at least send a $10 Starbucks gift card with a note that says, "Have a fancy latte on me!" This way, you're not supporting a political cause you disagree with, but you're still showing your love for your family member or friend. If you truly don't even have $10, you could also offer to help by saying something like, "I don't really have the cash to help you out, but I would love to put a sign in my yard, or help you deliver signs around my neighborhood." There are so many ways you can show your love, support, and kindness beyond money. As a candidate, you can also ask for these things. Ask your family members that don't want to donate if they could at least cook dinner one night a week, or pick your kids up from school. Ask a friend who can't afford to donate if she'll come over and fold laundry or do dishes for you. Remember, this is a scrappy campaign, and scrappy candidates need all the help they can get!

It's important for me to acknowledge that many of my friends and family did donate to my campaign and help me in many ways. Some of my biggest fans were my husband and my son, and a couple of good friends like Jennifer Empasis and Kip Hawley. My mom, my aunt, and my cousins were also great. We held what we called a "Miller Girl Weekend," where the women in my family got together to walk door-to-door for my campaign. My cousin and her fiancé made hundreds of phone calls for me from their apartment in Newport Beach from phone lists that I provided. Even my mom made calls to voters from her home in Ohio. This kind of devotion is priceless!

And some friends simply could not be stopped from helping. Kip showed up at every event. He even drove me to most events, and he always had a duffle bag in the back seat filled with snacks for me to eat on the way home (did I mention that I like free food?). Kip did anything and everything that was asked of him. He took photos at events, he took notes at meetings, he wrote press releases, he led debate preparations, he donated money, he walked door-to-door. He did it all! In many ways, he was my Ernie. Jennifer also helped out immensely. She was a friend who couldn't afford to donate, but she did everything else. She picked up my son, Bobby, from school and babysat when my husband had to work; she took him to karate class and cooked dinner; she washed dishes and folded laundry. She was my angel, and I was—and continue to be—so grateful for her friendship, love, and support. I asked way too much of her, but every time she came through and proved to be a great friend and supporter.

My husband, Bob, was my rock throughout the entire campaign. I remember when I first talked to him about running for Congress. When I asked him if he thought I could win, he said, "You can't win if you don't run." He was right. You will never accomplish your dreams if you're not willing to take a risk. If you're going to run for office, you have to be willing to be uncomfortable, be willing to sacrifice, and be willing to put yourself out there and take a risk. And it's true, you might not win. But you definitely won't win if you don't run!

My husband did something else that was important. Beyond supporting my campaign and cheering for me, he set an example for our son of how a husband supports his wife. He was by my side every step of the way. He took time off from work to be in commercials, he made dinner almost every night (even though most nights, I wasn't even home to eat that dinner), he took care of our son and did most of the shuttling to and from school and karate. And every night, he patiently listened to me talk about my laborious day. He was excited for me, and even when he wasn't, he acted like he was. In all of these ways and more, he demonstrated to our son that this was a real team effort.

The most important takeaway from this chapter is that you need to decide early whose support you want and whose support you need. I suggest that you definitely need the support of your partner and children. They don't have to be wildly excited about your race, and they don't have to agree to attend every event, but if they don't want you to run, then you probably shouldn't run. It really is a team effort, and your partner might become resentful if you're gone most evenings and weekends without his or her blessing. As for my husband, he's not a very social person, so I would always invite him to events with the understanding that it was completely up to him whether he attended. Our conversations usually went something like this:

Me: Honey, Jeanne and Ray are hosting a meet-and-greet tonight, do you want to come?

Bob: Will there be people there?

Me: Um, yes.

Bob: Then, no.

That's right, this is my husband's response to pretty much any invitation. If he has to meet people and make small talk, he doesn't want any part of it. I respected that and usually appreciated the fact that we didn't need to hire a sitter. Figure out what your partner's boundaries are, and respect those boundaries. Also, set ground rules about how much you want your partner to be involved in your campaign. My husband didn't have much interest in day-to-day campaign operations, but I've heard horror stories from campaign managers about family members who wanted to be invited to every meeting and approve all correspondence. This can be cumbersome for the staff and delay things that have to be taken care of quickly. My campaign manager was terrific when it came to my husband. My hubby had a habit of checking social media regularly and responding to comments about me. He was extremely protective of me, so if someone made a negative comment, he'd jump all over it. My calm 25-year-old campaign manager would simply send a text saying, "Delete that comment," at which point, my calm, patient, not-25-year-old husband always complied. We created a good rhythm that worked for our family and for our campaign.

A campaign can actually be a lot of fun when you are surrounded by people who love you and believe in you. You might not have the support of your entire extended family or all of your friends, but as long as your immediate family—the people you live with every day—are behind you, and you've got a trusted and loyal staff, you'll be just fine. Talk openly and honestly with your family, and let them know that you want their support, and that not having it will be very hurtful to you. Search for areas or issues where you can agree. And even if they can't help you financially, find other ways that they can show their love and support. Your campaign will likely last one year, but ideally, your relationships will last a lifetime. It's truly not worth ruining family dynamics or ending great friendships over a political campaign, and yet it happens all the time. This can be avoided. Engage your family and friends early in the process, recognize and respect different opinions, then show them how they can work with you toward shared goals.

And remember, someday, the naysayers will want to visit you in the White House, and you can tell the Secret Service to deny their request. I'm kidding . . . or am I?!

Lesson 5: Hire a Volunteer Coordinator and Other Key Staff

This chapter will focus on two critical points: 1) don't hire friends to work on your campaign, and 2) don't rely on volunteers in key positions. Every campaign book you pick up will have a chapter on campaign staff, and they will identify all of the positions necessary for a dynamic campaign. However, few of those books will paint a realistic picture of how the staff actually comes together and what their roles are. For example, some of the questions that I needed answered as a new candidate were, "How many paid versus unpaid people should be on my staff? How do I find people to work on my campaign? What should I do when one of those individuals is not the right fit?" Most campaign books include flow charts and organization charts depicting the ideal campaign team and appropriate roles for each person. But if you're running a scrappy campaign, you'll have to think creatively about how to get the work done with as few paid staff members as possible.

When I ran for city council, I used the same campaign manager, Alex, who had managed my friend's water district campaign. He was very knowledgeable about the local area and the issues, and he knew a lot of residents and donors. Because that was a small race, the only other staff that I had was my treasurer, who was a friend and volunteer, plus another friend who built my website and took photos for me throughout the campaign. Alex was the only paid staffer, and since the entire race only required about $5,000, he was paid $2,000. This is not much for a campaign manager, especially over a six-month period, but the truth is that I did most of the work myself, and he was primarily acting as an advisor. I'd call and ask him questions about donors or issues, and we met from time to time to talk strategy, but it certainly wasn't a full-time job. He probably put in about eight hours each month, so averaged about $40 per hour. He was the one who proposed this fee, so he must have thought that was a fair rate. Most campaign managers will tell you up front what their monthly rate is. Make sure that both you and the potential campaign manager have a clear understanding of how much the campaign will pay and how often, and put it in writing in a contract. Include a list of responsibilities, and have both people sign the contract. The faintest pen is stronger than any memory!

As a result of working on my friend's campaign together, and then working on my city council campaign, Alex and I became good friends. Naturally, when I was considering running for Congress, he was one of the first people I told. Honestly, he thought it was a bit crazy, especially since he was a

Democrat and I was a Republican intending to run against a Democratic incumbent. But over the course of a couple of weeks, we considered all the arguments and angles, and we both realized that it was a worthwhile endeavor. I was glad to once again have him on my team!

We kicked off the campaign in June 2015, and he agreed to be paid $2,000 a month initially, with that rate increasing to $3,000 and then $5,000 per month over the course of the campaign. One of the mistakes that I made was not drawing up a contract with the agreed upon roles, responsibilities, and compensation. Because we were friends, we simply talked about this and agreed to move forward. We had no other paid staff in the beginning. It was just the two of us travelling all over the district, meeting with voters and raising money. The only other person working with us was a volunteer and friend, Mike McMaster, who served as my treasurer. I also hired a contractor to help out with updating the website and social media posts. She cost between $500 and $1,000 per month, but this position didn't last long once we switched over to a more user-friendly and integrated website.

Because we were on a tight budget and trying to keep costs down, we didn't hire any other staff members. When we needed brochures and business cards printed, we paid the designer at the print shop to design them. I handled my own scheduling and event coordination. I wrote all of my own speeches and policy papers. Alex advised me on issues, introduced me to donors and business owners, and worked with the local media on behalf of the campaign. In the first six months, we had few volunteers and no finance committee. It was just Alex and me basically doing it all. As you can imagine, this was not a sustainable model for running a national level campaign! By early December, we were both exhausted and burned out. It was difficult for either one of us to conceive of how we could continue at this pace for another year.

In January, I met Kip Hawley, and he recommended hiring a national level campaign consultant. When I went to Washington, DC to meet him and the NRCC, it became clear to me that any campaign manager should have experience at the same level of campaign that you're running. Alex had run a lot of local and county campaigns, and he was outstanding on my local city council campaign, but he had never run a national campaign. Neither had I. The truth is that we were both winging it . . . and it just wasn't working. There was no way we could maintain the pace, do all the work ourselves, and be viewed as a credible Congressional campaign. I needed someone who could help me put together an organization of experienced professionals familiar with national campaigns. So I did what I had to do and Alex and I parted ways. Unfortunately, our friendship parted ways, too. Important campaign rule: don't hire your friends!

I went ahead and hired a national campaign consultant in February 2016. His monthly rate was $5,000! Yikes! That was a lot of money for my campaign, and he wanted me to hire a separate manager to run the day-to-day operations, a press secretary, a volunteer coordinator, and an attorney. Yikes again! I didn't have anywhere near the funds to run this type of operation. Okay, back to Chapter One and the importance of fundraising! It was probably not necessary to have a huge staff during those first six months, but it was absolutely necessary to raise a few hundred thousand dollars during that time period so that I could hire the four additional staff we needed in the spring of election year. Unfortunately, by that point in the campaign, I had raised only $150K, and I was saving every penny of that money for advertising.

I kept raising as much money as possible, every day and every week. Kip and I put our heads together to figure out how to come up with a reasonable campaign staff based on what we needed and what we could afford. This was the result:

Consultant: Chris ($5,000 per month)
Manager: Andrew ($5,000 per month; came onboard after the primary)
Press/Policy Advisor: Kip (free)
Treasurer: Mike (free)
Designer: Ren ($500 per month)
Scheduler/Admin: Megan ($1,000 per month)
Event Coordinator/Driver: Laura ($3,000 per month)
Volunteer Coordinator: Jennifer (free)
Social Media: Val (free)
Fundraising Chair: No one
Precinct Chair: No one
Photographer/Videographer: Robert (free)

Now let me explain what each of these people actually did, because in a scrappy campaign, people have to be willing to jump in and do whatever is needed. Often, that's much more than their job description. For each of the paid positions above, we had written contracts explaining the duties of the job, as well as the monthly pay. The treasurer and I signed these contracts, as did each employee.

Chris, our consultant, was located in Los Angeles, and he primarily consulted by phone, although he did occasionally travel to Monterey to meet with the team, help with debate prep, and attend the debates. He advised us on campaign messaging and how we should spend our money. If we were debating between doing a mailer or a radio ad, we would call Chris. He had the research and experience to know which was most effective. When we wanted to do a poll, he put us in touch with a polling company that offered us the friends and family rate because of Chris's connection. He also helped us create TV commercials, and choose the timing for commercials for maximum impact. He was a great help, and most months, he didn't even send a bill to us for his services (he even donated to the campaign). When we first met, I had asked him, if I agreed not to bug him too much, would he give me a discount? He said he would, so instead of talking daily, we usually talked weekly, and had very focused conversations in order to save time and money. Scrappy campaign advice: everything is negotiable, so negotiate rates with everyone on your staff.

Chris had recommended my campaign manager, Andrew, who was only 25 years old, but had previously managed a Congressional campaign. Andrew had also worked on various aspects of other national level campaigns. The great thing was, he was willing to move to Monterey for six months and dedicate his life to my campaign! This is so important. For any campaign, the candidate really needs to have a manager who lives in the same town and does not have another job or any other major commitments. During the last six months of the campaign, we worked about 12 hours a day, seven days a week, and I needed someone who was completely committed, and someone I could call or meet any time day or night. Andrew was that person.

The manager has a lot of different jobs, mostly managing the candidate, but Andrew was responsible for implementing the campaign strategy as well. He hired pollsters to conduct two polls. He hired a company to do opposition research on my opponent, and surprisingly, on me. Yes, you may indeed want someone to dig into your own life so that there won't be any surprises if, or when, your opponent does their own research on you. Andrew hired the advertising agency that shot all of our commercials and radio ads. He ordered yard signs and mailers. He managed the rest of the staff and led weekly team meetings. Generally, he kept us all on point and moving in the same direction.

I remember one meeting that we had after we received some polling information revealing the top issues in the district. Some of those key issues were water, transportation solutions, affordable housing, and healthcare. Kip and I love foreign policy and national security, so we were all psyched to write a press release about ISIS, proposing a national security plan to target terrorists and protect the homeland. This was a good time for the campaign manager to speak up, and Andrew did. Andrew reminded us that the poll findings showed that people in the district were not concerned about ISIS, they were concerned about housing and healthcare. He got us back on track and focused on what the people in our district wanted.

Megan was a young lady who worked in the Republican party headquarters. I convinced her to join my campaign and help out with scheduling. She was amazing! Megan was extremely organized and professional. I gave her access to my email and calendar so that she could go through requests, respond to them, and put them on my calendar if necessary. She also took notes at the meetings and kept track of who was doing what on our campaign. We got a lot of speaking requests, so she worked with Laura and Andrew to prioritize those requests and respond to them. There's also a lot of paperwork to fill out on campaigns. Every organization that is considering an endorsement asks the campaign to fill out a multi-page questionnaire. Once we had a general questionnaire completed, Megan was able to complete additional ones as required without having this be a major time-sink to me.

Laura was called our event coordinator, but she was so much more than that. Kip called her my "bodyman" because her real day-to-day duty was to be by my side wherever I went. Laura coordinated every single meet-and-greet and fundraiser we held, and sometimes there were four of these in a single week. She also drove me to every meeting, event, interview, debate, or anywhere that I needed to be. This was an amazing gift because, as a candidate, you can't be fiddling around with directions and trying to figure out where to go. You need to be able to just hop in the car, think about and rehearse what you are going to say, maybe catch up on some phone calls or emails, or even just have some quiet time. Laura was great about this! She was always on time, she was a safe driver who planned the route out in advance, and she let me pick the radio station. We listened to a lot of "Delilah" and spent a lot of time laughing and sharing stories during our time in the car together. Laura was also my personal advisor. She did my hair and makeup before TV shoots. She advised me on what to wear and what not to wear. These are the things male candidates don't have to worry about as much, but as a female candidate, it's important to create and maintain a certain image. I tried to strike a balance between professional woman and mom. Laura helped me do that.

Ren was our designer. He had amazing talent and was an all-around nice guy. He designed newspaper ads, mailers, brochures, signs, and kept the website updated. He even starred in one of my commercials. He was an extra set of hands to do whatever was necessary. He attended events and even helped clean up afterward. He walked in parades, delivered yard signs, and anything else we needed. Ren was a great team player.

Ren also worked with Val, who kept our social media up to date. I met Val through a mutual friend, and Val and I bonded immediately. She was a former Air Force intelligence specialist and a graduate student at Stanford. She was also a wife and mother of twin boys. For some reason, she agreed to help out with our social media, and she did it all for free! While we didn't pay Val, we did give her a budget so that she could put ads on Facebook and sponsor Twitter posts. She also made sure that we had consistency between Facebook, Twitter, YouTube, our website, and TV, radio, and newspaper ads. Val was superb in this role because she had a way of capturing my voice and putting into words exactly what I wanted to say, but she did it even better than I could. She worked with Andrew on the overall advertising plan, and she worked with Ren on the designs. Again, this was a real gift to have someone who was so talented, and such a true team player, to volunteer to work for free.

Kip did it all, and wasn't paid at all either. He was called my advisor and press secretary, but he did so much more. He was certainly my trusted advisor on any and every policy issue. He also helped a great deal writing issue papers and press releases. He helped me prepare for debates and media interviews. And, because of Kip, I can honestly say we won every debate.

Mike, our treasurer, was another person who was not being paid, but went above and beyond his role. Treasurer is a tough job, especially in a national race, because there are extensive Federal Election Commission (FEC) guidelines that must be followed. Visit www.fec.gov, and you will find a campaign guide for national candidates, and it's 198 pages long! My treasurer read this cover-to-cover and made sure we followed every federal election law to the tee. The reporting requirements are very cumbersome at this level, so you need a treasurer who is extremely organized and detail-oriented. This cannot be a shoebox operation! Mike actually purchased two separate laptops for tracking donations and filing reports. He downloaded special FEC software to file those reports, and he got to know the FEC staff on a first-name basis. Some people say negative things about the FEC, but Mike did not hesitate to call them when he had a question, and they were always very professional and helpful. The FEC provides a free version of the reporting software. We tried this initially, but it was not very user friendly, so we purchased another filing software that made some of the filing requirements easier. Mike also worked with Andrew on adhering to our budget. He controlled the checkbook and paid all the bills. Most importantly, he was ethical, and I never had to question whether we were adhering to the election laws. This is the one role on the campaign where, if you mess up, you can go to jail—both the treasurer and the candidate— so make sure you have the right person in this job.

Because the role of treasurer is so critical, legally speaking, you may not feel comfortable having a friend or volunteer fill this job. There are professional companies that perform the service of campaign treasurer. They will file all of the necessary FEC reports, maintain bank accounts, pay bills, and provide the campaign staff with 1099s. They will basically take care of all of the financial duties associated with a campaign. We looked into this option because Mike began to feel overwhelmed at one point when a lot of donations started coming in. I begged him to stick it out, especially because the professionals wanted to charge $4,000 per month to do what he was doing for free. Mostly, though, I trusted Mike and didn't want to hand this job over to anyone I didn't personally know and trust. At the end of the campaign, Mike did seek some professional help wrapping up the filings and ensuring that the campaign met all of our federal tax reporting requirements. This cost about $1,500 and was well worth it to ensure that we had closed out the campaign correctly.

Finally, Jennifer filled the role of volunteer coordinator. Her husband acted as our photographer and videographer at events. They both worked tirelessly, doing anything that was asked. Together, they delivered and installed nearly a hundred 4 ft. x 8 ft. campaign signs. Jennifer spent a lot of time reaching out to schools and other organizations to solicit volunteers. There were hurdles around every corner, and we fell short of our goals time and again. Based on my experience, I'd recommend that this is one job where you really shouldn't rely on a volunteer. It wasn't fair for me to ask Jennifer to take on this role. Instead, it is likely you will need to hire a professional volunteer coordinator. People who have experience in this role know where to find volunteers, how to place them in the organization to get the most out of their contributions, and how to motivate and retain them. Jennifer had every good intentions, and she worked her butt off, but it's hard work and it's a full-time job. Don't forget that Jennifer was also helping me at home as well! If I had to do it all over again, I would hire someone to fill this full-time position. I truly don't know what I would have done without Jennifer and her husband. They stepped up to help me and my campaign in a huge way.

When it comes to volunteers, you can never have too many. There are oodles of things these priceless team members can do to help. We definitely needed more people canvassing and phone banking. We needed help delivering yard signs and walking in parades. We needed someone to write letters to the editor and work the farmer's markets. We needed college students staffing tables on every college campus in the district. There is an unimaginable amount of work on any campaign, and I was grateful for every paid and unpaid member of the team who jumped in and helped out. Managing all of these volunteers and field operations is an enormous job that simply can't be left to one person, and certainly not even to one very capable volunteer. Bottom line, my recommendation is to hire a professional and experienced volunteer coordinator. If you can't find or afford one, then hire a campaign manager who has previous experience in this position on another campaign. I'm deeply grateful for everything that Jennifer did, and I'm lucky she's still my friend, considering everything that I asked of her.

Running a campaign is much like running a small business. You have to hire and fire people. You have to develop a budget and raise revenue. You have to brand and market your product, the candidate. You have to identify target goals and milestones. And you have to make adjustments along the way. Be flexible! Don't keep doing something that isn't working, and don't keep someone on your team who isn't the right fit. If you have to fire someone, do it and move on. Be clear at the beginning, middle, and end of your campaign about what your expectations are, and lead by example. I expected people to work hard and be committed to the campaign. But above all, I wouldn't settle for anything less than ethical and professional behavior.

If you do face an ethical dilemma during your campaign, face it head on. We had one incident in which someone on my staff got hold of my opponent's debate binder. My opponent had left it lying on the table after a debate, and my staff member picked it up and handed it off to another staffer. When I got wind that it was in our possession, I was furious! I immediately called my opponent, told him what happened, and got it back to him ASAP. I never did see that binder, and I don't think anyone on my staff even looked inside it, but this was still a breach of ethics in my view. The incident was resolved within an hour when my campaign staffer met with my opponent's campaign manager and handed over the binder. My opponent handled the incident graciously. That's all there was to it. Still, it was certainly questionable behavior and I didn't like it one bit. I didn't fire that person because I chalked it up to being young and inexperienced. Afterward, I pulled my team together to discuss the incident and reiterate my expectations that all of us hold ourselves to the highest ethical standards.

This was the only incident like that that we dealt with over the course of an 18-month campaign, and it turned out not to be much of an incident at all. When my campaign was over, I was exhausted, but I was also extremely proud of my team. We had all worked hard, and we had worked well together. We made hundreds of good decisions, and we could hold our heads high knowing that we did our very best, and we did it the right way.

Lesson 6: Organize Your Time Geographically (and Avoid Vomit)

Before I ran for city council, someone told me, "Time and money are the most important elements in any campaign. You can always get more money, but you can't get more time." Here are a couple of key takeaways when it comes to managing your precious time: 1) it's okay to say no to an invitation, and 2) it's NOT okay to say no to free press. Sometimes saying no can actually make you look better than showing up someplace under less than ideal circumstances. When I was running for city council, my son was two years old, and my husband and I were both working full time. The Chamber of Commerce was hosting a reception for business owners to meet the candidates. I really wanted to go, and I wanted to show off my family. My husband had less than zero interest in these types of events and my son was cranky, but I convinced my husband that we all three should go for a short time, then go out for pizza afterward. He reluctantly agreed. When we got to the reception, there was a dessert table and, of course, my husband and son headed straight to that table while I mingled around. Apparently, my son ate a lot of sweets on an empty tummy, because the next thing I knew, he was at my feet asking to be held. I was surrounded by business owners and thinking this was going to be the perfect demonstration of me as a mom: I'll pick up my adorable son and hold him while I'm talking about important small business issues. So I leaned down to pick him up, and just as I got him up to waist level, he threw up all over me! Then he started screaming! I rushed him to the bathroom to get him cleaned up and give him a drink of water. As for cleaning up myself and making a re-appearance, it was hopeless. I was a mess! I grabbed my husband, and we got out of there as quickly as possible. I was mortified! But perhaps it wasn't as bad as I thought. Someone later told me that I probably got the votes of every mom, dad, and grandparent in the room. After all, anyone who has kids has probably been thrown up on . . . more than once!

Sometimes it's better to just decline an event rather than attend and face disaster. Another embarrassing incident happened at the start of my Congressional race. I was doing laundry on a Friday afternoon and carrying way too much stuff when I lost my footing. I fell down two steps and twisted my ankle. After a not-so-quick trip to the ER, I found out my foot was broken. The downside was that I had plans to go to the county fair the next day to meet all the big-wigs in the agricultural industry. I was determined to go anyway, but I could barely walk, so I limped all over the place. At one point during the day, I was invited up on stage and introduced as a veteran and candidate for Congress. Limping up on stage, I waved to everyone. When I came off the stage, many people approached me and thanked me for my service. That's when it occurred to me that they probably thought I was a disabled vet. No, I'm not a disabled vet, I just can't seem to carry a laundry basket down two stairs!

By fall, our campaign was in full swing, and I got invited back to the same county fair. My son had a karate competition that day, so I decided to go to the competition and miss the fair. It was more important that I support my son, but I also worried that all of those farmers might be really disappointed to find out that I'm not disabled, I'm just clumsy. Plus, by this point in the campaign, I felt more comfortable declining requests to show up at every event known to man.

Candidates are invited to speak at a lot of events, walk in parades, set up tables at festivals, participate in chili cook-offs and salsa contests, judge car shows, and somehow squeeze all of this in while meeting donors, making fundraising calls, and preparing for debates and candidate forums. Below is a partial list of the organizations that invited me to speak during their monthly luncheons. This list reflects only those I actually attended. There is another equally long list of organizations which I declined simply because my schedule wouldn't allow it.

Old Capital Club	Sustainable Monterey	Big Sur Advisory Council
Stillwater Club	American Legion	Successful Thinkers
Rotary (every city)	PEO	United Vets Council
Deputy Sheriff's Assoc.	VFW	Young Farmers
Business Council (each county)	Chamber of Commerce (every city)	Growers and Shippers
Republican women's club	Ministerial Alliance	Coast Property Owners Assoc.
Firefighters Assoc.	PTA (every school)	Fresh Fruit Assoc.
Republican Central Cmt (each county)	Navy League	Maggie's List
Farm Bureau (each county)	Women's Lawyer Assoc.	LULAC
Realtors Assoc.	Cattle Women	County Medical Society
Hospitality Assoc.	Yacht Club	Kiwanis
	Federal Employees Union	

With some of these organizations, I could use my standard pitch about who I was and why I was running for office. But most of these groups wanted a speech that was specific to their members, which requires far more preparation time. For example, the realtors wanted me to lead a conversation about property tax deductions, federal loan programs, and the importance of home ownership. The firefighters wanted me to talk about fire breaks, protecting pensions, national guard support, and federal grants. The Big Sur Advisory Council was focused on short-term rentals, which was a local issue, not a national one, but I still had to be prepared to speak about it. Each of these events required research, writing a speech, and practicing the speech. There was rarely an event where I could just hop in the car and go without any preparation.

In my Congressional race, we also had at least one debate or candidate forum each month during each of the last eight months of the campaign. Of course, we knew the major issues in advance, but any topic could come up, so these events also required a great deal of preparation time. Because there are so many requests for the candidate to speak or attend events, and since time is limited, it's best to organize your time geographically. Have your scheduler and campaign manager map out what the next couple of months will look like, and in which part of the district you'll be spending your time.

In the district where I was running, there were about 26 cities within three counties and part of a fourth county. One way to organize time in this situation would be to plan in advance to spend a particular day each month in one of these 26 cities. Then if you get a request to speak at the San Benito County Farm Bureau, for example, your scheduler can say, "She will be in that area on August 5th." Otherwise, you may end up driving from one end of your territory to another in a single day, wasting a lot of time on the road instead of meeting voters. Here's a look at a typical schedule for one of my days during our campaign. This was a good day because, except for the last meeting of the day, everything was in the same city.

```
6:30-7:30: emails
8-10:00: Farm Day at Monterey fair grounds
10-12:00: make donor calls
12:00: meet donor for lunch at Hyatt
2:30: meet campaign manager
3:00: Meet donor
4-6:00: meet-and-greet in Monterey
7-8:00: Farm Bureau meeting in Salinas
(home by 9:00)
9:30-10:30: emails
```

Unfortunately, we weren't always this well organized, and sometimes Laura ended up driving me from one end of the district to the other in a single day. There were days when we left my house at 6:00 am and didn't get home until 10:00 pm. Below is my schedule for August 11, 2016. We were in four cities in three counties in one day. Yes, this was a real day.

```
6:30-7:30: emails
9-9:15: press interview w/KSBW (Pacific
Grove)
9:30-10: issue brief mtg
11:15-12:30: Ladies Day lunch at Casa Amesti
(Monterey)
1:45: ballot due to elections dept and meet
Hollister city council members
5:30: Gilroy Chamber event
(home by 8:30)
9-10:00: emails
```

Life would be great if your schedule worked out exactly as you planned, but what often happened was a national event or a local incident would occur, and the press would call and ask for an impromptu interview. Of course, they always wanted it done quickly so they could shoot it, edit it, and get it on the five o'clock news. Every time candidate Clinton or candidate Trump said something provocative (which was quite often for the latter), I was contacted and asked to make a statement, so this happened a lot. There are events that you can turn down, but one thing you should never say no to is free press.

On one occasion, Laura and I were driving from meeting to meeting, going in all different directions, when I got a call requesting an on-camera TV interview. Scrappy campaigns are campaigns on a tight budget, so if you can get on TV without paying for it, definitely don't pass up that opportunity! I told the reporter where I was, and she happened to be headed in the opposite direction. Finally, we decided on a location midway where we would meet and conduct the interview—on the side of Highway One in Moss Landing. We met in a parking lot alongside of this busy highway and did the interview with the traffic hurtling by at high speed. It seemed as if every time I started to answer a question, an 18-wheeler would whiz by and completely drown me out. There are definitely better places to do these ad-hoc media events than on the side of the road!

Speaking of organizing time and managing speaking requests, one important thing to think about is who will have access to your calendar and who will be authorized to add things to it. In my case, Megan (scheduler), Andrew (manager), and Laura (events) were all authorized to add things to my calendar, but everyone on our team could view it so that they knew where I was at any particular time. This feels very strange if you're not used to others controlling your schedule. I couldn't wait until the campaign was over so I could go out and buy an old-fashioned paper planner and not share it with anyone!

Another consideration is what events you should go to and which ones you can decline. My criteria weren't always explicit, but generally, if my opponent was going to be at an event, then I had to be there as well. Second, if media would be present, then I needed to be there. Third, if there was an opportunity to raise money, I went. Sometimes after I spoke at a Rotary luncheon, some of the club members would hand me campaign donations. If I thought I could meet my daily fundraising goal in this way, I'd go. Finally, if there was an opportunity to get an endorsement from a particular organization, I'd go. For example, the Firefighters Association or the Realtors Association meetings were definitely worthwhile because I wanted to demonstrate my commitment to them and my knowledge of the issues that were important to them. When a campaign gets a request for the candidate to attend an event, it's always worth asking about the agenda and how many people they expect to attend. If there will be 100 people there, that's a great crowd worth getting in front of. If there will only be 20 people, and the majority of the meeting will be organizational business, then you may want to consider declining their request.

Keep in mind both your daily fundraising goal and your energy level. If you decline an event in order to meet with donors, and you can raise a few thousand dollars from them that day, that money can pay for a TV ad that will reach thousands more people than you could have met at most events. In addition, it takes a lot of energy to prepare for and participate in daily events. Be mindful of your energy level and schedule in downtime during each day if possible, and definitely at least a few times during the week. There are certain things you should proactively schedule during a campaign, like dinner with your family at least once each week. I also scheduled a date with my husband one evening every month. We tried to schedule days off, usually Wednesdays, but it was extremely difficult for me to take a whole day off knowing there were people I should be meeting and money I should be raising. Usually, those Wednesdays would end up being light days, which would give me an opportunity to catch up on emails or phone calls, or simply go to the grocery store.

The bottom line is, guard your time. The campaign manager should help protect the candidate's time as much as possible. Time really is a precious commodity in any campaign. Many people will want to meet with you. Many organizations will want to hear you speak. It's okay to say no. It's okay to take a day off. It's okay to choose your family or your child's event over a campaign event. If you do attend an event, make the most of it—try to get a press report or a large donation from every single one. And remember, wherever you go, smile!

3 The Realistic Side of Public Service

"What is noble can be said in any language, and what is mean should be said in none.
— *Maimonides*

Lesson 7: The Media (Not Your Campaign) Controls the Narrative

Oh, the media—we love it and we hate it! We love the media when their reporting about us is positive, and we hate it when the reporting is negative or unfair. Get this through your head: the only time you can control what is said about you on TV or in the newspapers is when you are paying for it. The majority of your campaign budget should be spent on advertising, not on paying for staff or office space. Invest your precious campaign budget in TV, radio, and on-line advertising. This is the only way you can control the narrative of your campaign and the race in general.

The reality of politics is that your campaign is largely dependent on the media. I remember one debate that we had prior to the primary in which I outperformed my opponent in a big way. I had thoroughly prepared, typed up notes, and rehearsed repeatedly. This was our first debate, and I wanted to prove myself and show that I was a serious candidate. After all, I was running for the US House of Representatives! The debate was hosted by the Santa Cruz Chamber of Commerce, and about 200 people were in attendance, including a reporter from the local newspaper. I was so excited when it was over, because I felt that I'd done well, and I couldn't wait to see the press reports the next day. However, I was disappointed to see that the newspaper reported that both candidates performed well, that we were both knowledgeable on the issues, and we both had impressed the audience. From my perspective, that wasn't true at all! I realized right then and there that the media was not going to be fair and unbiased in this race.

Deciding to be proactive, I requested a meeting with the editorial board of that local paper. There were actually two county newspapers, but they shared the same editor and had significant overlap of people on their editorial boards. In one of the meetings, there were four people in attendance, one of which worked part-time for my opponent's father, and another whose husband worked full-time for him. Now, do you think this was a newspaper that could be impartial and objective? I was not convinced that they could be, but I had one main purpose in proposing that meeting, so I stayed focused. I wanted them to endorse two candidates in the primary. Since there were five candidates running, and the top two would go on to the general election, I figured they had some wiggle room when it came to making an endorsement in the primary. They didn't have to support only one candidate. They could recommend to their readers which two candidates they believed should move on to the general election. Mission accomplished! They didn't agree immediately, but when their endorsement came out, they did endorse both my main opponent and me. I was thrilled!

There were also a few other local newspapers that interviewed all five candidates for possible endorsements. I tried the same tactic with them, but with no success. The other papers endorsed my opponent, but one of them ran a front-page cartoon of him riding a tricycle to Washington, DC with his mom and dad waving goodbye. It wasn't very flattering to say the least. Of course, I was disappointed not to receive their endorsement, but it also demonstrated that the media could be cruel and unfair to all candidates, not just me. After that cartoon came out, there were consequences to the paper from my opponent's campaign. The following week, their editor wrote an article titled "Musings on the election, witness protection, and what comes next," in which she admitted, "I went to bed that night with one thought: Sylvia is going to kill me!" (Sylvia is my opponent's mother).[5] Fortunately, my opponent's mom did not kill the editor, but she did call her to complain about the cartoon. How embarrassing is that?! Note to self: don't complain to my mom and don't *ever* let her call the local press. Ever! I don't know what was more embarrassing, the cartoon of the tricycle or the fact that his mom called the newspaper to complain.

Photo credit: Monterey County Weekly

---

[5]Monterey County Weekly, May 26, 2016.

Family, friends, staff, and especially the candidate, need to be completely prepared for the fact that the press will report things that may not be true, they will print unflattering pictures, they will make cartoons about your campaign, and they will generally make your campaign harder, not easier. I had a good relationship with local reporters on TV and radio, and also with the newspapers, but I still found it astounding when, after a 20-minute interview, they would select one thing I said and use only that one quote in their entire news report. This is why it's so important to research the topic before you conduct a press interview. Write down a few specific points. Practice what you will say. Make each point short and quotable. And be careful to stop talking once the interview is over. Don't engage in small talk! If you do keep talking after the interview is over, you risk letting something slip that you don't want to see in the news. If you simply must chit chat afterward, always be positive and keep smiling. These unrehearsed statements and candid clips might just end up on the five o'clock news.

If you're fortunate enough to have a press secretary on your staff, that person will have certain contacts in the press and a general list of contacts of where to send press releases. However, the candidate and campaign manager should also have a separate list of press contacts, preferably newspaper editors and TV producers. There were times I wanted to get a particular message out, and I didn't want my comments to be treated like the myriad other press releases that crossed their desks. With these contacts, I was able to call the decision-makers directly and ask them for coverage. Sometimes it worked and sometimes it didn't. I was also able to call or text these folks to request a correction to something that had been printed incorrectly. You may think it's obnoxious to call an editor or producer directly to ask for press coverage, but if you're on a scrappy campaign, you need to do whatever you can to get in front of the cameras. Don't be shy about approaching the press! There is a law called the Communications Act, also known as the "equal-time rule," that pertains to election press coverage. This law requires that broadcast stations give each candidate equal time. It also requires that, if purchasing advertising, both candidates are charged the same rate and provided the same opportunity for prime-time slots.

When it comes to radio and TV, radio ads usually run in 60-second segments, while TV ads are purchased in 30-second time slots. Sixty seconds allows you time to tell a story about you as the candidate and why you're running. It's also enough time to allow you to connect meaningfully with voters and tell them how you will address certain issues. According to a study done at American University, 74% of those surveyed felt that radio was an important source of political information.[6] The important thing is to select the best radio station for maximum voter contact. Each station knows their audience numbers and their ratings, so you will know exactly which segment of the population you can reach during various times of day through your radio advertising.

Television typically has a greater reach than radio, but is also quite a bit more expensive. Being on television can legitimize a candidate and a campaign quickly and effectively. Like radio, the television market has been thoroughly researched. There's plenty of data available about exactly how your swing voters spend their viewing hours. Industry tracking firms know who is watching what content, all broken down by age, education, voting history, income, location, and gender.[7] You can purchase this data, and it will be well worth it if you are trying to target a certain segment of the population through your TV ads.

One of the major expenses associated with TV advertising is hiring a production team, including someone who will video, edit, and produce the ads, as well as work with the TV stations to get your commercials on the air. A poorly crafted television spot can hurt your campaign, so don't cheap out when it comes to producing an ad that tens of thousands of people are going to see. Often, there are community access stations hungry for programming, so they might agree to produce a show with the candidate, or provide a set for commercial production at minimum cost. Whoever you hire to produce your ads, remember that those ads won't just air on TV. You'll want to be able to post them on YouTube, Facebook, your website, and other online platforms. Make sure your contract with the advertising agency includes this kind of holistic approach. Having advertising on each of these mediums allows you to control the narrative of the campaign despite other news interviews or clips that may not have captured and communicated your main message.

One effective way to control your message in print media is through letters to the editor. At the beginning of your campaign, put together a committee of volunteers willing to write such letters. These committee members should also agree to find additional volunteers who will submit these letters. You can have the initial committee members draft the

---

[6]"Americans Speak Out About the 2000 Campaign," conducted by the Center for Congressional and Presidential Studies.
[7]Catherine Shaw, *The Campaign Manager; Running and Winning Local Elections* (Westview Press, 2010), 239.

letters so that your message is consistent, but you can't have the same five people always sending in letters. That's why they need to have other people willing to put their names on the letters and submit them to the print media. Sometimes at an event, someone might approach you and ask how they can help on your campaign. Of course, it's great to get a donation, but you can also ask them to write a letter to the editor. If they agree, put them in touch with someone from your letter-writing committee. Start this effort early because, as the campaign goes on, readers become numb to the endless letters and political reporting.

In your letters to the editor, focus on the issues that are most important to local voters. Use these letters as opportunities to highlight your strengths. These letters enable others to speak on your behalf, and they can brag shamelessly about the solutions you've developed for ongoing challenges without you appearing to lack humility. Don't have the authors defend you or attack your opponent. Instead, have them draw specific distinctions on things that matter, such as experience and expertise. Keep the letters polite and professional. Doing anything less risks the paper rejecting them.

Another way to control your message, as the Russians have taught us, is through social media. Obviously, you need to keep your website updated because that's probably the first place people will go to check you out. But the next place they'll look will likely be Facebook, Twitter, Instagram, or YouTube. Make sure you have consistency between these mediums. Think about one thing that you want people to remember about you, then reiterate that through all media channels. Perhaps you want people to think, "Casey Lucius, she's going to address the drought and other water issues," or, "Casey Lucius, she is a veteran and a mother." Whatever it is, select your primary message and stick with it. This way, you stand a better chance of attracting people who are aligned with your message, rather than confusing voters and risk becoming less memorable.

This was probably one of my campaign's greatest shortcomings. We had so many themes that we wanted to focus on, but we never consolidated this into one core message. I wanted people to know that I was a professor, wife, mother, and veteran. I wanted them to know I would address local issues like transportation, water, and affordable housing. But I also wanted them to know that, since I was running for a national office, I understood budgets, national security, and foreign policy. Whew, that's a lot of stuff for anyone to remember, even me! Guess what? No one remembered any of that, or at least this broad message didn't resonate with most voters. On the other hand, my opponent had one simple message: "I'm from here." Period. It was simple, and it resonated with constituents. Voters liked the idea of voting for someone who was one of them, and it clearly distinguished him from me because I wasn't from that area. Keep it simple, and repeat it over and over again, in every forum and at every opportunity. Of course, you have to address the issues that are important to people, but you can include your core message with each answer: "I'm from here, so I know we need highway improvements. I'm from here, so I've experienced the impact of the drought firsthand." Kudos to my opponent and his staff because that was an extremely effective message! Next time, I'll know.

There are certain things in a campaign that no one can control. Once you realize this, it will be a lot easier to let things go and focus on what you *can* control. There will always be somebody who can find something to criticize about anything and everything you do. You could make the best commercial known to man, but someone will still find something about it that they don't like. You can post all positive messages on social media, but there will still be people who respond with negative posts. It's not even political, it's just human nature. I once did a TV commercial intended to appeal to women and mothers, so we did the shoot in my own kitchen where I was packing my son's lunch while saying the script. The ad turned out great, but someone wrote a letter to the editor complaining that I had used a plastic Ziploc bag rather than a more environmentally-friendly, reusable container. Geez! Of course, they were right, but come on, people! Probably no one remembered what I actually said in that ad, they only remembered that I used a darn plastic bag for my child's grapes!

We all know by now that social media can be divisive and down-right nasty. It can be a great political tool for getting your message out, but your campaign should also have a social media policy that includes guidelines for reading and responding to comments. I decided early on that I was not going to read comments or online newspaper articles, but for some reason, I still read Facebook and Twitter comments. As a result, I sometimes wasted an enormous amount of time reading and responding to comments on these social media channels. If you have a press secretary, ask them to take on this task. Val would often respond to Facebook comments with tact and diplomacy, which was wonderful, but that never seemed to stop me from jumping into the fray to make my point to some random person online. Don't do it! It only makes you look petty and provokable.

There is a big difference between mean comments on social media and threats. Unfortunately, my campaign did receive a few threats, and we encountered some worrisome incidents, which I'll talk about in the next chapter. One of these occurred on Twitter, and it was serious enough for us to put in a place a security plan and file a police report. It happened after a national interview with Fox News and my appearance on the Bret Baier program. I had made a comment on air saying that I didn't support Trump's immigration plan because it would not work well in my agricultural district. (Immigration crackdowns repeatedly leave crops rotting in the fields in California.) Later that night, I received several tweets criticizing my position, but there were three in particular from one person who referenced "Muslim male savages" who would love to rape a woman like me. The language itself was alarming, but what really concerned me was not knowing who the person was who made the posts. Did he live down the street from me, or did he live in another state? Was he really a threat or mentally unstable? We didn't have these answers, so we decided to report it to the police, who then worked with Twitter to find out exactly where that person lived. It turned out he lived in another state, but our local police department worked with the police in his area to ensure that he knew that threatening a federal official is a felony (technically, I was not a federal official, but I was a candidate for federal office and that message was effective).

Most people who run for public office are Type A people—they're go-getters, driven perfectionists who like to be in control. This is certainly true in my case. In 2013, David Rosen wrote an article identifying six personality types typically found in those who run for public office. They're not at all flattering: 1) narcissistic, 2) obsessive compulsive, 3) Machiavellian, 4) authoritarian, 5) paranoid, and 6) totalitarian.[8] For people who like to be in control, campaigning can be difficult, but it's also a great learning experience. I grew both professionally and personally from my scrappy campaign adventures. I gradually came to the realization that there were many things I couldn't control in our campaign. I couldn't control what the press said about me or what pictures they printed. I couldn't control how the Republican party treated me. I couldn't control the negative comments on social media, and I couldn't even control my own daily schedule. This can be a real challenge for us control freaks! I come from a family of alcoholics, so I'm intimately familiar with this prayer used throughout AA.

---

[8]David Rosen, "The Six Political Personality Types", Campaigns and Elections, October 6, 2013.

"Grant me the serenity to accept the things I cannot change, the courage to change the things I can, and the wisdom to know the difference."
—*Reinhold Niebuhr*

I recommend committing this wise advice to memory and muttering it under your breath daily while on the campaign trail. It really helps!

Lesson 8: There Is a Political Machine, and It's Not Friendly

I strongly believe that the political machine consists of money, the media, political parties, and the intimidation and hypocrisy associated with political campaigns. I've talked a little bit about each of these already, and I'll go into more detail about money in politics in the next chapter. Here, I want to paint a realistic picture of how brutal campaigning can be. I don't write this to discourage anyone from running for public office. Rather, I've decided to include this chapter because there is so much you must know going into a campaign that no one will ever tell you. It's kind of like having a baby. When people approach a pregnant woman, they congratulate her and tell her what a blessing it is to be a mother. No one says, "Oh my God, it hurts like hell to give birth, it takes weeks to heal, and months to feel like yourself again. And you'll be exhausted for the next three years!" Why doesn't anyone say this? It's all true, but it's only part of the story. Being a mother *is* a blessing, just like running for office is an amazing opportunity. It's exciting and fun, and a great learning experience. But it can also hurt like hell, take months before you feel like yourself again, and you'll be exhausted for years, especially if you win!

Let me share a few of my experiences during the campaign that I wish someone would have warned me about so that I could have been better prepared. A lot of things happened on the campaign trail, but it was the hypocrisy that surprised me the most. I was a woman running for office in the "Year of the Woman." This was an exciting time! It was a time when we might have the first woman US President, and the first woman to represent California's 20th District. Neither of those possibilities came to fruition. I learned the hard way that women don't vote for women candidates just because they're women. We talk a good game about supporting and empowering women, but the truth is, people vote based more strongly on party affiliation than gender affiliation. In fact, in 2016, more women turned out to vote than men. The Center for American Women in Politics at Rutgers University conducted a study in July 2017 of voter turnout in elections from 1980–2016. In 2016, 63.3% of women reported voting compared to 59.3% of men. So, if women voted for women, and we elected our president based on the popular vote instead of the Electoral College, Hillary Clinton would have won the 2016 US Presidential election. Most voters vote based on party affiliation, not gender preference or important issues. Actually, I'm glad that women voters are thoughtful, and not just voting for women merely because they are women. But voting for a Republican or a Democrat primarily because he or she is a Republican or a Democrat is really no different. As voters, we need to think more deeply about why we are casting our vote for a particular candidates. We need to dig into the issues and ethics of each candidate before we make our decision about who to support in the polls.

Not only was I unpleasantly surprised that more women didn't support my candidacy, especially in the Year of the Woman, but I was also taken aback by how many women were critical of my candidacy. This applies both to my experience running for Congress and when I ran for City Council. In 2012, during my Council race, I went to a women's luncheon and gave a speech about local issues and my positions on those issues. At the end of my talk, I took questions, at which point, one of the ladies said, "Shouldn't you stay home and raise your son instead of running for office?" I'm not kidding, someone actually said this to me in the 21st century! My answer was, "This is how I'm raising my son. I'm showing him the importance of public service. I'm showing him that, instead of just complaining, we have to get involved and present solutions. I'm showing him that we sacrifice our time to make contributions to our community. I'm showing him that his mother is a strong and independent woman." Any other questions?

That wasn't the last time I got that question. When I ran for Congress, nearly every debate or candidate forum included a question directed only to me, regarding how I planned to balance my family commitments with the travel that would be required if I won the election. People would ask if we planned to move to Washington, DC so that I could continue to fulfill my parental responsibilities. My opponent also had young children, but he was never asked this question. Shockingly, it's still not easy for some people in our society to wrap their heads around the idea of a mother going out working and travelling while the father stays home to take care of the kids. Even some women have difficulty accepting this as a viable option.

Maybe it was my optimistic nature, but I also expected to receive support from women Republicans in Congress and conservative Republican leaders in California like Condoleezza Rice. In addition, I wrongly assumed that women legislators at the state level would step up to show their support for a female candidate. None of these women at any level came through for me. Perhaps they didn't like me, or maybe they just didn't want to support my campaign for whatever reason. Fair enough, but as women, we do need to decide whether we want to see more women in office, and if we do, let's put our money where our mouth is! Let's stop talking about it, get moving, and start helping qualified women who put their names on the ballot.

Once a local reporter asked me why I put my picture on my large yard signs. He suggested that I only included it because I was using my looks to get preferential treatment. In fact, I put my picture on those signs because I have a gender-neutral first name, and I wanted voters to know that Casey Lucius is a female. By the way, the picture on the sign wasn't an advantage, in part because voters don't vote based on gender, but mainly because hoodlums drew mustaches on my face or horns coming out of my head. Ouch! There was also one incident in which someone drew a penis on my sign and spray-painted the word "Whore" across my face. On another sign, someone painted boobs on my chest. You can't really do much about these kinds of attacks, and you can't control them. But they really irritated me because, like the "good mom" questions, I knew these were annoyances that only female candidates were likely to encounter. No one was painting "whore" on my opponent's signs. (I was tempted to add a tricycle to his signs, but I resisted.)

One of the most important issues we face as a society today is how women are treated in the workforce. The #MeToo movement has provided an outlet for many women to share their stories of gender harassment, abuse, and violence. It has also provided an opportunity for women to encourage each other to no longer tolerate those types of working conditions. It's hard to believe that we're still dealing with these types of injustices in 2018. Women in campaigns are encountering the same things that working women endure. What are we going to do about it? I'd never advise a woman to vote for a candidate based on gender alone, but I implore both women *and* men to support qualified women candidates in order to help put an end to the nonsense that many women put up with in their professional lives.

I hoped to never utter the words "good ol' boy," but the truth is, I was fighting against the ultimate good ol' boy network. I've come to believe that the only way women will make headway in politics, in Hollywood, in the media, in the military, and in many professions, is if we kick down the door to the good ol' boy clubhouse and let men in leadership positions know that more is required of them on the issue of gender. Now, don't get me wrong. I don't want to kick men out of their jobs or out of public office, but I want them to know that our standards must change, their leadership style must change, and women must be treated fairly and equally. As Reese Witherspoon's organization says, "Time's up"! We mean it, and we expect results.

Throughout our campaign, people tried to intimidate me into dropping out of the race. In addition to the threatening tweets, negative comments on social media, biased press coverage, and vandalism, I also had my car keyed from bumper to bumper while it was parked in the driveway at our home. It's amazing how vicious people become regarding politics. I was not expecting any of this. I had quit my job to run for Congress. I thought people would thank me for stepping up and making this sacrifice for our community. I imagined that people would appreciate me for taking the time to learn the issues and offer thoughtful solutions. I hallucinated that people would respect me for being ethical and running a clean campaign. (Did I mention that most candidates are narcissistic? Me too, I guess!) It sounds ridiculous even to me now, but I did consider myself a great candidate, and I thought everyone else would see me that way too, even if they chose not to vote for me. That was certainly not the case! Please don't expect people to thank you or be nice to you when you're a candidate. It's not that you don't deserve this kind of civility, it's to protect yourself from disappointment and discouragement when you're the target of this kind of behavior. If there's one good thing about egotistical people, it's that they bounce right back—and that I did, over and over and over again!

The political machine also includes the influence of political parties. I already mentioned that I assumed Republicans would support me because I was Republican. The voting data says this is largely true, but only if you appeal to your base, which is where I missed the mark. Nevertheless, I was proud to earn the endorsement of some leading local Republicans. There were also some prominent business leaders, especially in the agricultural industry, that supported me and in spite of the influence of my opponent and his famous family members. However, there were also prominent Republicans who initially endorsed me only to call me later to ask to have their names removed from my website. This happened with two local mayors who endorsed me early on in the campaign. They later said that they couldn't have their names associated with my campaign because they were nervous about the implications. What implications? From who? Was the party intimidating them? Was my opponent pressuring them? Maybe their mothers were concerned about my parenting duties? They declined to explain their reversal. What do you say when someone endorses you and then un-endorses you? All you can do is respect their request, ask for an explanation, and ask them to vote for you anyway. I had to remind a lot of people that, while their endorsement was public, their vote was private.

When the vandalism, threats, and reversal of endorsements didn't work, the opposition went after my husband. Bob spent 23 years in the Marine

Corps, and he's a vegetarian and an animal lover. After his time in the military, he transitioned to the nonprofit world and began advocating for animals. Someone from my opponent's side generated a false email about my husband, saying he was a vegan who worked for the Humane Society and that he was the mastermind behind my campaign. The email suggested that, if I were elected, my husband would draft policies that would hurt farmers. It was complete and utter nonsense! My husband is a long-time vegetarian (as am I), not a vegan. He did work for Humane Society International, primarily on a Green Monday campaign in Asia. His work had nothing to do with farming practices in the United States. Nevertheless, this phony email was sent to farmers throughout the district, and it significantly hurt my campaign. Up to that point, I had the support of many in the agricultural industry, but after this "fake news," it was difficult to convince them that my vegetarianism or my husband's work to protect animals would not impact their business. It all seems quite silly in retrospect, given that we lived in the Salad Bowl capital of the world, and I was a vegetarian, promoting eating more veggies. Be prepared for these types of underhanded attacks against the candidate and their family. Yes, we've seen this type of illegal and unethical activity occasionally in presidential campaigns, but it can still be a bit of a shock when it seeps into our neighborhoods and our own races.

There were also several organizations that refused to endorse in this election at all. I was rarely given an answer about why they weren't endorsing, so I could only assume that it was because they didn't want to get involved and face the possible blowback if they made the "wrong" decision. Like those mayors who withdrew their support, there were certain organizations such as the Farm Bureau, CalFire, and the Hospitality Association that chose to stay out of the fray. Not endorsing at all was better for me than if they had endorsed my opponent, but staying neutral is a position that lacks principle. In my view, I had the courage and tenacity to jump into this race, so the least these organizations could do was have the courage to state publicly who they thought was the best candidate. It wasn't clear to me why they wouldn't, but it was perfectly clear that there was some underlying intimidation going on that was quieting their voices.

The best thing any campaign can do in the face of intimidation, media bias and political games is to stay focused on the day-to-day operations of the campaign. As the candidate, my primary job was to raise money and connect with voters. My campaign manager worked to keep the rest of our staff motivated and focused. The staff and volunteers needed to make brochures, design mailers and ads, call voters, be at the farmer's markets, deliver yard signs, write press releases, update social media, and get out the vote. We were able to use some of these negative incidents as media opportunities, or as a reason to ask volunteers to write about them in letters to the editor, but mostly, we needed to ignore these tactics and keep pressing forward.

Negative campaigning is part of the political process. In some cases, it works, and in other cases, it doesn't. In one ad, I stated that my opponent shouldn't be elected simply due to his family name or because of his father's credentials. It wasn't that negative, but it was shot in black and white and had eerie music playing in the background, so it had a negative vibe to it. It didn't work. I should have known better. Numerous studies conducted on the impacts of negative campaigning show that only four areas consistently fall into fair territory: 1) voting record, 2) ethical problems, 3) business practices, and 4) money from special interest groups. Attacking someone's name or family connections doesn't resonate with voters, and bringing my opponent's father into the race was no different than them dragging my husband's diet into the fray.

When negative things do happen in your campaign, call a meeting of your core team to let them all know what happened and decide how you will deal with it. Make sure everyone knows what to say if the press calls. The answer may be as simple as, "This is very unfortunate, and we have no other comment." Not every attack has to be responded to, but you must be prepared for negative attacks, and even imagine possible scenarios in advance.

As I've mentioned, my expectation for my staff was that people work hard and be committed to the campaign. But above all, I expected ethical and professional behavior. During these kinds of difficulties in our campaign, I constantly reminded myself of two things. First, we all needed to stay focused on these core values. Second, I reminded myself of why I was running. I was running for many reasons, but I needed to stay focused on my belief that it was time for a woman, for a new generation, for someone with a middle-class background, and for new ideas, to inhabit this leadership position. I was running because I had something to contribute and wanted to serve my community. When you think about the big picture like this, the tweets, the nasty sign vandalism, the hurtful emails and comments, all fade into the background. Yes, you need to be prepared for these kinds of incidents, but you also need to rise above them. Stay true to your purpose, and keep your team focused on the new ideas and the professionalism that people deeply desire, and that our political system desperately needs.

Lesson 9: Money Is Evil—But It's Legal

Yes, money is necessary. Chapters One through Five have all touched on the need for money in order to run an effective campaign. A local campaign may only require $5,000. A national campaign might cost anywhere from $500,000 to $5 million. The reason that I say money is evil is because it's not only used to run the campaign operations, buy data and advertising, and pay for staff. Money is also used to buy the media's goodwill, secure political favors within the party, purchase negative advertising, intimidate voters, and more than a decent human being can imagine. Let's discuss how you can raise and use money to support your campaign, and remain aware of how money can be used against you. It is impossible to avoid money in a campaign, but we can learn from others—role models like Bernie Sanders, whose average donation was $27. You should also be on alert against illegal uses of campaign dollars, and know your rights and reporting requirements associated with the financial engine of politics.

It's always revealing to discover where candidates get their money and how they spend it. If you're like me, you're probably wondering how a campaign could possibly spend $200 million. I can't imagine raising or spending that much money, but it's done every couple of years all over the US, in governors' races, Senate and House races, and presidential races. In the 2016 Presidential race, Hillary Clinton raised an astounding $1.4 billion and Donald Trump raised $957 million! Even Bernie Sanders raised approximately $234 million that same year.

What's more is that all of these candidates had significant financial support from Super PACs. Most of us think "Super PAC = bad news," but let's dig in to see what a Super PAC really is and whether they are beneficial to the political process or not. A PAC is a political action committee that raises more than $1,000 to influence an election, and each PAC must register with the Federal Election Commission (FEC) and follow certain election laws. There are also PACs at the state level that support candidates running for state and local office, and these organizations are bound by state laws which vary from state to state. There are "connected" and "non-connected" PACs. For example, when I ran for City Council, the Firefighters Association sent out a mailer on my behalf. They paid for the mailer through their PAC, which raises money from their members. This is a "connected" PAC because all of the money received comes from people connected to that organization. Connected PACs usually have a specific platform, and contribute to candidates who will support their business sector. Non-connected PACs can collect money from any individual or group, and they don't have to be connected to a particular organization in any way. They typically focus on a single issue or ideology that they want to support.

Another type of PAC is a Leadership PAC, which is usually implemented by a sitting politician. For example, Congressman Paul Ryan could only personally donate $2,700 to a candidate's congressional campaign, but his Leadership PAC could donate an unlimited amount to that same campaign. The only caveat is that the candidate cannot coordinate or communicate with the Leadership PAC.

Then there are Super PACs. Generally, the public hates the idea of Super PACs collecting and spending money to influence the outcome of elections. Super PACs came into being in 2010 after the *Citizens United* Supreme Court decision declared that PACs could collect an unlimited amount of money from individuals, unions, and corporations in order to fund their independent expenditures. "Independent" is the key term here. According to the FEC, there must be no coordination between the candidate, campaign, or political party and the Super PAC in determining how money is spent for or against a specific campaign.

The difference between a PAC and a Super PAC are the contribution limits. During my Congressional race, I received contributions from PACs, including one called Women Under Forty PAC (WUFPAC), which donated $1,000. I also received a donation from Maggie's List (the Republican equivalent of Emily's List), and they made the maximum allowed contribution of $5,000. According to the FEC, a PAC can donate up to $5,000 to a candidate annually, and they can discuss how to spend that money with the candidate. In my Congressional campaign, three PACs donated to my campaign: WUFPAC, Maggie's List, and Granite Construction PAC. They all donated directly to my campaign, and we could spend that money anyway we wished. With a Super PAC, it's different. They can collect unlimited donations and spend money on campaigns as they wish with no limitations whatsoever. Money from a Super PAC is not considered a contribution, and a campaign is not responsible for tracking it or reporting it to the FEC.

Whether you think Super PACs are good or evil, almost every candidate running for office hopes that some white knight on a horse will come along and fully fund their campaign, or at least make their fundraising challenges a bit easier. In politics, that white knight is a Super PAC. I was hustling every day to raise money, and only in my dreams could I hope that someone would come along and drop $1 million into a PAC to help my campaign. Dreams sometimes come true, and this kind of happened . . . a little bit. A Super PAC called American Freedom Builders Action Network (AFBAN) independently paid about $50,000 to create and air a commercial supporting my campaign. It was a terrific commercial with the theme of how important it was to elect women in 2016. I thought it was outstanding, and I didn't feel one bit guilty about having this Super PAC try to influence the election. My race gave the term "underdog" a whole new meaning, and I needed all the help I could get.

I did, however, get a lot of flak from my opponent, and from the media, for using what they termed "dark money" in my campaign. Technically, I didn't use any of this money. I didn't see it or touch it. The intention was that I would simply benefit from an ad that someone else paid for, created, and put on the air. While there was a lot of criticism of my campaign regarding the $50K from the AFBAN Super PAC, my opponent had collected well over $300,000 in PAC money, mostly from Washington, DC interest groups. It infuriated me that his PAC money, enormous by comparison to what was spent on our behalf by the AFBAN, was deemed acceptable while mine was not. While he was quick to criticize me on the Super PAC issue, he was simultaneously supporting Hillary Clinton, who had over $200 million in Super PAC money spent in support of her campaign.

Voters would be better off, and campaigns would be cleaner, without Super PACs, and perhaps without any PACs at all. In 2016, my opponent received about $100,000 from union PACs, $37,000 from registered lobbyists, and $28,000 from Leadership PACs. We both benefited from the contributions of PACs, but I think it would be more ethical if the members of those organizations donated directly to the campaign instead of doing it under the umbrella of a particular business sector. The problem as I see it is not that receiving money from a PAC is bad, but that there are expectations that the organization places on the candidate to support their agenda in exchange for their contributions. The winning candidate is expected to vote on legislation that supports that PAC's specific industry or issues. As an example, my opponent received a large donation from a sugar PAC located in Florida. Personally, I love sugar, and I have nothing against the sugar industry. But he was elected by the people of California's 20th district, so my hope is that he'd make decisions in the best interest of CA-20, not those of sugar producers in Florida.

Ideally, we'd create laws that limit PAC contributions, as well as out of state contributions, but this isn't likely to happen because it infringes on our First Amendment Rights. According to the CATO Institute, the First

Amendment protects both political speech and the resources (money, printing, the internet) to facilitate that speech. In 2002, the McCain-Feingold law limiting the amount of political contributions any individual could make in a two-year period was passed. For 2011-2012, an individual could contribute up to $46,200 to all federal candidates combined, and $70,800 to political action committees and political party committees, for a total of $117,000. Such limits have been debated in the courts for years, and this law was eventually overturned based on the argument that restrictions on campaign spending put a heavier burden on political expression than on other types of expression, one which the government could not justify.

Despite our individual rights to donate money and collect campaign contributions, there are many ways money can be used illegally in the political process. As a national candidate, you are bound by the Federal Election Commission. As mentioned in a previous chapter, the FEC provides a 198-page guidebook detailing all of the rules and regulations concerning raising money, spending money, and reporting campaign fundraising and expenditures. For local or state campaigns, visit your state's secretary of state website to find out what your state regulations require. Look for a section called Elections or Campaigns. There, you'll find campaign finance rules, as well as other helpful information on running your campaign in accordance with your state's election laws. You'll also want to spend some time reading through the candidate qualifying information and voter registration statistics (see Chapter Two on knowing your numbers). There will also likely be a helpful guidebook intended for the campaign treasurer, so they will know exactly how to file the necessary reports accurately and on time. And there will be a number of forms that need to be completed in order to register your committee (yes, you will be establishing a Political Action Committee, a PAC of your own!), as well as all of the forms required to get your name on the ballot. Every state and municipality is different—in some cases, you'll need to collect a certain number of signatures to get your name on the ballot, and in others, you can bypass the signatures and simply pay a fee. Usually, you can also pay to have a personal statement inserted on the ballot next to your name. This is a great opportunity to convince voters to vote for you. Of course, it all costs money. Even filing the forms with the state usually involves paying a fee. In any case, start the process early because you'll need time to either collect signatures or solicit contributions to complete the process of being listed as a candidate for office.

At the local, state, and national level, there are also forms and official mechanisms by which you can lodge a complaint if you feel your opponent (or any candidate) has violated the campaign finance laws. Be aware that literally anyone from the public can file a complaint, so it's best to stay above board, keep accurate records, and report all fundraising and spending properly.

There are so many finance rules and reporting requirements that simply skimming through the FEC guidebook may discourage you from running for office. But don't be discouraged. Think about some of the people who get elected, and remember, this is not rocket science! If you do feel overwhelmed, ask your treasurer to read and be responsible for all of the sections concerning financial reporting. The candidate and campaign manager can then be responsible for allowable contributions and prohibited spending. You will also want to familiarize your finance committee with these rules. There are some obvious limitations on how campaign funds can be spent. For example, don't use your campaign contributions to pay for personal rent, home utilities, or college tuition. You also can't buy clothes with this money—remember Vice Presidential candidate Sarah Palin in 2008? A big no-no, the Republican National Committee spent $150,000 on clothes for her and her family to wear during the campaign. Another no-fly zone: don't spend campaign funds on entertainment like sporting events or music concerts—think up-and-comer Aaron Schock who gave up his Congressional seat in 2015 and was later indicted on 22 counts, including filing inaccurate reports to the FEC, corruption, and fraud.

Money in political campaigns is necessary and legal, but it can definitely lead people down the wrong path. Unfortunately, if elected, campaign contributions corrupt the way our elected officials vote on legislation. As candidates, it can also influence the way we conduct our campaigns. Money can be used to buy favor in the media or in your political party. But you can also use money to communicate an important message—a message that inspires people and gives them hope. You can use money to touch as many voters as possible, letting them know how you will tackle the problems they are facing. Decide early on how much money you'll need to raise and how you'll raise it. Consider carefully whether you want to accept money from PACs. If not, challenge your opponent to do the same. Don't split hairs on whether it's PAC money or Super PAC money. If you decide not to utilize PACs, then don't accept *any* kind of PAC support.

It might be risky, but you could even set a personal campaign contribution limit for your donors. Perhaps you could use a past candidate as an example, and announce to the public that you will not accept more than $50 from any one donor in your race. This could mean you pass up a lot of larger donations, but it could also attract a horde of voters who've had it with financially motivated corruption, as well as some donors who may not otherwise donate to your campaign. In an age when many voters are frustrated with politics and disgusted by the amounts of money used in political campaigns, this could be a very attractive message. You can also be creative about your campaign spending. For example, if you have a large homeless population in your county, perhaps you announce that your campaign will donate $50 to a local shelter or food back for every $100 spent on campaign advertising. Again, these strategies can be risky, but things will never change unless we take action to change them. It's time to think outside the box when it comes to raising and spending money on political campaigns. If we really do want these customs to change, it will require individual candidates to make tough choices and meaningful changes for the better. Why not start with your campaign?

4 The Substantive Side of Public Service

"Make no little plans; they have no magic to stir men's blood...Make big plans, aim high in hope and —work." —Daniel H. Burnham

---

Lesson 10: Whether You Win or Lose, You Will Win *and* Lose

A few months after the US Congressional race, I was asked to be on a panel to speak about women's empowerment. One of the other women on the panel happened to be my former opponent's wife. She's a Superior Court Judge and all-around intelligent, impressive woman. I hadn't seen her or talked to her since before the election, so I walked over to say hello. She had always been kind to me, even during the heat of the campaign. I asked her how things were going and how her husband enjoyed his new post in Washington, DC. She said something about being exhausted—not him, but her. She was now at home, mostly on her own, working full-time and raising their two daughters. I realized at that moment that perhaps *I* was the winner in that race. I lost the election, but I got to continue living in my home with my son and my husband. The "winner" of the race had to travel back and forth to Washington, DC each week, leaving his family behind and relying on his wife to pick up additional family duties. This was an aha moment for me. I realized that losing a race might mean winning in certain ways, while winning might mean losing parts of life that are precious.

Winning an election will change your life, as will losing an election. Either way, your life will never be the same. Since I'm an optimist, let me start by sharing with you some of the things I gained by running for office and how my life was changed for the better. Both in my city council race and my Congressional race, I gained knowledge. I learned about community issues and challenges. In particular, on the city council, I learned about sewer laterals, infrastructure planning, desalination plants, stormwater runoff catchment systems, airport land use, and more. I could go on and on about the local issues that city councils and county commissions tackle on a daily basis, but what was even more interesting to me was learning about political processes. I had studied political science in college, even earning a PhD in political science, but nothing really teaches you about the political process as well as sitting in that leadership position making policy decisions. On the City Council, there were only seven of us, unlike in Congress, where there are 435 representatives, and not one of us could pass any legislation, or achieve anything, really, without majority support. We followed all of the state's public meeting laws and took public comment at each meeting. We weighed the views of the public with the realities of the budget. We debated revenue options and alternatives to cutting spending. We negotiated with public employee unions to ensure fair pay and benefits for the city staff. I learned more during the one year that I campaigned and the four years that I sat on the Pacific Grove City Council than I did in 10 years of higher education.

I also learned a great deal about leadership and building consensus. There were times when I was faced with a dilemma where I had to choose between my personal preferences and what was in the best interest of the community. There were times when the vote was 6-1 and I was the sole dissenter. And there were times when the vote was 7-0 because I was able to make a convincing argument to my colleagues that got them to vote with me. At times, the public was happy with my decisions, and at other times, they were unhappy and very critical. I got both good press and bad press during my tenure on the City Council. I also learned patience and when not to speak up. I learned just because you have an opinion, that doesn't mean you have to share it. We had long meetings in which I had to be exceedingly patient with the public and with the other council members. Patience is not one of my strengths, but serving in a public role and being required to listen to others and be thoughtful in my own decision making certainly has strengthened this quality in me.

I also gained new friends and met business leaders and community members. I formed a strong bond with our mayor and another council member. The three of us didn't always see eye-to-eye on the issues, but we had a great respect for each other's intellect and the process by which we each made decisions. I also gained a new respect for small business owners who are often negatively impacted by the policies made at the local level. Business leaders are a unique bunch because, not only do they live in the community and have their own concerns as residents, but they are also trying to run a successful business, hire employees, provide a service, attract new customers to town, and generate revenue, which in turn generates revenue for the city. Small business owners are a bit like military members—they make a sacrifice because they believe in something bigger than themselves, and in return, they face challenges and receive few assurances about their future. If you've ever walked up to a service member to thank them for their service, consider doing the same with your local business owners. They're not risking their lives, but they are making meaningful contributions to the local community through their business leadership.

In running for Congress, I had similar opportunities to learn and grow. In addition to learning about broader issues, I met some amazing residents and made lifelong friends. Running for Congress required a different level of skill because it involved understanding local, state, and national issues. Not only did I have to understand the challenges surrounding healthcare and immigration reform, I also had to be able to speak to those points concisely on camera, debate them knowledgeably, answer questions off-the-cuff, and put my solutions in writing for all to see. Previously, I mentioned that I wrote over 26 issue papers for my campaign website. I also prepared and presented my solutions on dozens of topics at candidate forums and organized events. My learning curve was steep, but by the end of the campaign, I felt confident that I could speak intelligently on any topic, make a logical argument, do a press interview, and debate with even the strongest opponent.

Most of us have some opinion on major political issues. For example, if someone asked what you think about the 2018 tax reform bill, you could probably say one or two sentences about it and give your opinion for or against it. But someone running for office has to be able to do more than share their opinion. They have to know the facts about the bill, what aspects are beneficial for different sectors, and what parts of the bill could be improved upon. They must know enough not just to form an opinion about an issue, but to answer tough questions about that issue. They need to be able to speak about it live on TV without stumbling over their words. Because of my campaign experience, I can now do all of this with confidence on any issue, given enough prep time.

Another great thing about running for office, despite occasional negative media reporting, is the opportunity to build a credible reputation. If you are strong on the issues, articulate, and come across in a professional manner, people will grow to respect you, even if they don't vote for you. I accomplished this in my Congressional campaign, and even more importantly, I generated credibility for the Republican party. No credible Republican had run for that district seat in decades! But now people in that community know that the Republican party does have young, smart, female candidates who can and will challenge the status quo. I earned a reputation as someone who was gutsy, as well as professional and polished. People say some unflattering things about political candidates, but I consider ending the election being described as gutsy and credible a huge win!

Finally, I gained new friends and true friends. I've already talked about a few of the wonderful people who contributed in some way my Congressional race. I've also talked about the disappointment I felt when confronted with the lack of support I received from certain groups and a few individuals. But the truth is, it's extremely touching when someone you don't even know sends a donation or writes you a letter of encouragement. It's amazing when a friend hosts not one, not two, but three meet-and-greets for you, and gives you tickets to every event possible so you can go mingle and garner more support. The people who stood by my side or came onboard during the campaign were my lifesavers. I couldn't possibly thank them all individually. There were 1,108 people who donated to my campaign. There were hundreds of people who wrote me notes of encouragement, called me to check up on me, and kept me in their thoughts and prayers during the campaign. After the campaign was over, I put all of the press reports into two binders, and filed all of the letters and cards (and even sticky notes) I received into a scrapbook. Looking through that book the other day, I found this note:

Dear Casey,

Thank you so much for running for the Congressional seat in our district. You have been a strong current of fresh air in an otherwise predictable, dull political climate here in District 20 where we seem to attract lukewarm performances.

I have enjoyed watching you gather momentum, squarely face issues, then use your impressive knowledge, honesty & directness to offer ways and means to solutions.

I have no doubt of your capability to eventually face the nationwide problems that have led to this circus tent election in the upper levels.

I am very proud of you, and even myself for being a vocal supporter.

Thank you Casey for stepping up.

James Radicchi

This type of support meant the world to me, and reading these inspiring messages got me through some of the toughest days of our campaign. In fact, when I sat down to write this part of the book, I started feeling melancholy, as all of the emotions from the campaign came rushing back to me. The heartbreak that I felt on election night hit me again as I started to outline this chapter. I decided to take a break, went into my little office, and checked my email. To my surprise and delight, there was a message there from a complete stranger asking me if I planned to run for Congress again. His email made my day, and it came at just the right time! He explained that he and his wife had never voted for a Republican before, but they both voted for me because, even though we would have disagreed on certain issues, they would have been proud to be represented by me in Washington.

There are certainly many heartbreaks during a campaign, especially a large, national one, but there are also moments and people who warm your heart, lift you up, and remind you that this is an important endeavor and overall, a wonderful life experience. I lost the election, but I gained much more than a seat in Congress. In fact, as the 115th Congress took their seats in January 2017 and proceeded to vote on over 700 resolutions, and eventually, a government shutdown, I realized once again that maybe I was the lucky one. Maybe I wasn't meant to be there, in the midst of all this negativity and dissention. I wondered if God was somehow protecting me by not sending me to Washington, DC. I lost, and yet, in this way, I won. Okay, I'll admit it, I would have rather won the race! But there's nothing wrong with digging for treasure when life serves you up a big pile of disappointment!

While I may have won the personal victory of not engaging in the mess that is Washington, DC, the bottom line is that I still lost the election, an election I truly wanted to win. And I lost badly. If the results were close, I may have considered another run and tried again. But the results were a landslide in favor of my opponent. It seems clear that I wasn't supposed to go to Washington or be in Congress, not at that time or in that district anyway. But there's always another election, so who knows!

U.S. House, California District 20 General Election, 2016			
Party	Candidate	Vote %	Votes
Democratic	Jimmy Panetta	70.8%	180,980
Republican	Casey Lucius	29.2%	74,811
	Total Votes		255,791

Source: California Secretary of State

This campaign took nearly 18 months out of my life. My son was five when we started and almost seven when we ended. I missed a lot of time with him while I was traveling all over the district raising money and trying to get votes. I've heard people say that they are running for office for their kids, so that their kids can have a better future. My advice is, if you are doing it only for your kids, then don't do it! The best thing you could do for your kids' future is to be present for them during the precious time they are with you at home. Read with them, play with them, and spend time teaching them. I missed the nighttime tuck-ins, the after-school homework, the karate and baseball practices, and dozens of other experiences that I can never recapture. At the time, I rationalized this sacrifice by telling myself that the campaign was important, and I still believe it was. Whether or not they have children, every candidate has to make sacrifices. Unfortunately, I sacrificed time with my child in order to run for Congress. That is time I will never get back. But just as I said during my city council race, I believed I was setting an important example for my son and I will continue my community involvement whether in an elected position or not.

The campaign also took a toll on my family in other ways. With a little help from friends, my husband was left to take care of our home, do all the shopping and cooking, take care of our son, and work at the same time. I was tired while campaigning, but he was tired from pulling double duty at home. Since I had quit my job as a professor to run for office, our checkbook also took a beating. Our income was basically cut in half. We knew this would happen, and we had prepared a budget to ensure that we could afford this decision. We could still pay our bills, but our quality of life absolutely suffered. Not only did we not have much family time, but we also didn't have extra money for dinners out, gifts, or anything else out of the ordinary. By the time the campaign was over, we had completely depleted our savings. We decided not to use personal funds to pay for the campaign, and absolutely not to go into debt. Nevertheless, living along the California coast is expensive, and without two incomes, we couldn't make it work. Because of my decision to run for office and the subsequent loss, we ended up selling our house and moving to a less expensive area. I carry a lot of guilt for my responsibility for this decision. We moved out of our town to another state, left our home (the first home we ever owned), made our son change schools, and uprooted all of our lives. This was all so I could run for office. Was it worth it? Well, I'm a big believer that you can't tell good luck from bad luck when it's happening. I may not know for years whether it was the right decision, but living with no regrets is quite a challenge during an experience like what we've gone through after I lost the election.

Running for office is simultaneously very selfish and selfless. On the one hand, you're putting yourself out there as a potential leader for the betterment of your community, ideally because you want to serve your constituents. Yet, nearly everything about the campaign process is focused around the candidate. My husband and son had to rearrange their schedules around my schedule. We dramatically rearranged our finances to enable me to run for office. Volunteers gave their time to support me. Donors gave their money. It's challenging to come to terms with all of this, especially when the outcome is not a successful election. I share this because, if you do lose an election, of course you will feel disappointed, but the weight of that disappointment will be multiplied because of all the people you've let down by your defeat.

Now that I've had time to reflect on the campaign and its outcome, I realize that I gained a lot and lost a little. Primarily, I lost time and money. The money I can earn back, the time I cannot. More importantly, I didn't lose my integrity or my character, which are core to my being. I didn't lose my desire to serve in public office. Surprisingly, I didn't lose my love of politics, in spite of all that I experienced. What else did I lose? Perhaps my innocence. Next time I run for public office, my son will be older, and I will be much wiser thanks to this adventure. As frustrating as it was, I still watch the news every night and track votes in Congress. I still go to county meetings, so I know what's going on in my area. And I still volunteer on advisory boards so that I can contribute in some small way to the process of decision making in organizations whose cause I support.

These are all things to think about before you commit to your campaign. Determine what you are willing to lose, and even more importantly, what you are *not* willing to lose in the campaign experience. Make sure your immediate family members have a say in this as well, and are completely onboard with your decision to run, as well as your guidelines for your life on the campaign trail. Set expectations about what specifically you expect of them, and in particular, what they are unwilling to endure. When the campaign's over and the dust settles, there can be resentment among people who are personally impacted by your decision to run.

On election night, when the results came in and it was clear that I'd lost, I called my opponent and congratulated him. It was one of the hardest calls I've ever made. But in addition to wishing him well, I promised him that I would do anything that I could to ensure his success in office. He was very gracious. He complimented me on a well-run campaign and he said we put up a really good fight. When I hung up the phone, it hit me that, suddenly, it was done. After 18 months of fighting, hustling, fundraising, interviewing, smiling, speaking, debating, and agonizing—it was finally and completely finished.

I made that phone call alone, outside. When I walked back into our election night party, I went to the microphone to announce that it was all over. This was another tough moment, but this moment wasn't about me. It was about my team and all of the people who supported our campaign. I thanked them all and let them know that night's party wasn't about the election results, it was to celebrate them and honor their hard work and uncountable contributions throughout the entire campaign. From the heart, I told them how much I appreciated each and every one of them and their priceless support. And then we celebrated. In spite of the outcome, we celebrated.

The morning after the election, I woke up with a splitting headache. No, I wasn't hungover. In fact, I didn't drink at all during the party. I think it was stress and anxiety that had built up over the past weeks and months. My husband made me a delicious breakfast, and then I went for a massage with my mom. We decided at the last minute that it would be a great way to escape from the world, at least for an hour. (Is there anything that a massage can't improve? If so, I haven't found it yet.) I relaxed, knowing that the most important people in my world were still by my side, and I would survive this as I've survived so many other challenges in my life.

Do It Anyway!

Before I jump into all the reasons why you should still run for office despite my lessons and warnings, let's do a quick summary of what we've covered in this book.

The 10 Lessons I Learned on the Campaign Trail:

1. **Donations** — Know how much money you need to raise to run a successful campaign (look at prior campaigns in that district), have a plan to raise that money, and put a finance committee in place before your campaign begins.
2. **Numbers** — It's worth paying for accurate voter data. Also, consider voter demographics and registration before you launch your campaign (remember how gerrymandering can predetermine election outcomes).
3. **Party Support (or Not)** — Decide early on if you want or need the support of your political party, and determine what concessions you're willing to make to acquire and maintain their support.
4. **Family Support (or Not)** — Politics is very divisive, even in families. Figure out whose support you absolutely need (i.e., your children, life partner, and other immediate family members), and consider support from other relatives a bonus.
5. **Staff** — Pay for the right people with the right level of experience. Demand professionalism and ethical behavior from every single person associated with your campaign.

6. **Organize Your Time** — It's perfectly fine to decline invitations, but never turn down free press. Spend most of your time raising money and being in front of a camera.

7. **Media Control** — The media is unfair. Get over it! Figure out how to get the most and best press coverage through both personal contacts and paid advertising.

8. **The Machine** — Scrappy candidates will not be intimidated into dropping out of a race. It's part of the game. Don't take it personally, and don't get your feelings hurt. Just grow a bigger backbone and keep fighting the good fight!

9. **Mo' Money** — Know your reporting responsibilities, and set personal standards regarding PAC donations.

10. **Winning and Losing** — Get ready to win *and* lose regardless of the outcome. You will lose time and money, but you will gain experience, exposure, connections, and relationships regardless of the outcome.

Now on to substance, standards, and strength! If you have read this entire book, then you already know that there are plenty of reasons why running for office is daunting and risky. Similarly, there are a host of reasons why people would rather watch the news and complain than stick their necks out and run for office and work to change things. The world of politics is hard work—there's no doubt about it. Running for any political office is difficult, discouraging, exhausting, and all-consuming. But our cities, counties, states, and our country need good, smart, motivated people as our political leaders. So, if you feel a burning desire to serve in this way, do it anyway!

Personally, I'd encourage anyone who reads this book to either put your own name in the hat, or work on a campaign to support a candidate you believe in. If you're not yet sure this choice is for you, consider these three major benefits of running for office: substance, standards, and strength. These are not just benefits for the candidate or the campaign team, these are the benefits our society will experience if we initiate positive changes to our political system and improve the campaigning process.

Let's start with substance. Please raise your hand if you would love to hear a political debate or television ad that focuses on issues rather than rhetoric and personal attacks. Is your hand in the air? Good! Mine is too! I have to say that it seems that we've reached a new low in this country when it comes to personal attacks during campaigns. But the historical truth is that the earliest political attacks were those made in 1796 against our first president, George Washington! An anti-federalist newspaper at that time warned that our nation was being deceived by a "debauched" George W. In 1856, a member of the House of Representatives literally beat a Senator with his cane because he had said something disparaging about South Carolina, the Representative's home state. And in 1964, Lyndon Johnson ran an ad literally suggesting that we all might die in a nuclear holocaust if we didn't vote for him. That was two years after the Cuban Missile Crisis, and Johnson's team was appealing to voters' fear and emotions, a tactic that continues to be used in recent times. Johnson's ad was controversial and distasteful, but Johnson won. Manipulating people through fear works, but shame on those who stoop to this level to get elected.

More recently in our presidential campaigns, we've heard candidates make fun of one another's height or the size of their hands, as if either of these characteristics had any bearing on their ability to lead this country. We've seen women judged based on their physical appearance and the suits they wear. This kind of negative advertising and offensive campaign tactics have made a mockery of our political system. We live in a country where every citizen can exercise their right to vote, and where anyone can put their name on the ballot for consideration as a candidate. This is a precious part of our freedom. I've lived overseas, so I know firsthand that this is not the case in many countries around the world. While living in Vietnam for three years, I learned that each citizen does indeed have the right to vote, but there is only one name on the ballot, so that "right" is severely limited.

In America, we are not limited, and we should not allow a corrupt political process to limit us to choosing between the "lesser of two evils," especially when it comes to electing people to top leadership positions. We must demand substance in our political campaigns. Let's not be limited to sound bites on the news or 140-character tweets! Instead, let's demand that candidates dig into the issues and answer questions that go beyond party talking points. If you are a candidate, or participating on a campaign, set this standard for yourself. Research the issues that are important to voters, and take time to deeply explore the problems and possible solutions. Thinking back to the issues in my own race in California, we were facing a long-term drought and needed new sources of water. Some of the options being debated were building desalination plants, mandating more conservation, digging wells, and purchasing water rights from other jurisdictions or federal lands. There was nothing about these potential solutions that was either Republican or Democrat. They all had merits and they all had risks. As candidates in that race, we had a responsibility to focus on the specific and diverse needs of our cities and then determine the solutions that our residents could afford. To me, the debate was one of substance, not politics.

Think about the issues facing your city today, write down the main problems, and then generate three or four possible solutions. Go in search of different perspectives to ensure you really understand the problems at hand. Debate the pros and cons of each of the possible solutions for each problem on your list with your campaign team. Dive into the details, do the research, and seek to truly understand the depth of the situation for each problem, as well as the overall system and context influencing the situation. Then, in your advertising, public speaking, and debates, you will be able to speak to these issues at a level that most Americans have not seen nor heard. You can engage on these issues from a place of expertise rather than perceptual bias and cognitive distortion, something to which human brains are exceedingly susceptible. Rather than being political, let's focus our campaigns on being substantive.

Next, let's grapple with the concept of standards. I've talked in this book about setting standards for yourself and your campaign staff. I have always held high expectations for myself and those around me. I require hard work, commitment, and honesty from anyone who works with me or for me. I absolutely demand ethical behavior. It doesn't mean people can't make mistakes. Lord knows, I've made lots of mistakes, and this book is chockful of them! But, just as we need to be substantive in our campaigns, we also need to raise our standards and our expectations for our own behavior, those around us, and our opponents. Challenge your opponent to run a clean campaign. Go to the media together and announce that both of you commit to stick to the issues and avoid personal attacks.

You can set a standard with the media as well. One tactic used by the media is to try to lure you into a discussion about your opponent. Make clear to them that there are certain topics that are off-limits for you. Set this standard and maintain it, no matter how tempting the topics might be. If you are determined to run a clean campaign, stick to your commitment and don't take shortcuts. Some people may offer you an endorsement or a large donation in exchange for saying or doing something that they want. Stick to your personal and professional standards, and don't compromise them for anything or anyone. When your campaign is over, whether you win or lose, you will have your integrity and your character intact.

You can also set a standard for raising money. Consider making a public statement at the beginning of your campaign listing the organizations or companies that you will not accept money from. Ask the public to hold you accountable to this pact. Similarly, set a standard with your political party. They may want you to endorse another candidate or support a specific position in exchange for their endorsement. Decide how you truly feel about that person or that position before you accept the endorsement. Can you do it without compromising your standards? If not, don't do it! It's time to start running a different kind of campaign. It's time for candidates to stop relying so heavily on their Party's support or Super PAC funding, and start appealing directly to the voters. It's the voters who have a say in the outcome of every election. We must not allow any party, PAC, or company to take away the influence and decision-making power of our citizens. It's time to put democracy back into our democratic process.

Finally, let's bring a new level of strength to campaigns. I'm talking about growing a backbone, people! If you're serious about running a campaign based on substance, standards, and strengths, then you must be gutsy and scrappy. You need to let people know that you are serious about winning your race. If you are a woman running for office some people may tend to underestimate you, or label you as "only a wife and mother." Others may try to intimidate you into dropping out of the race. Don't run away. Run anyway! Do not be deterred. Stick to it and show everyone how strong and scrappy you truly are.

When I think of strong women, I think of my hero Amelia Earhart, the first female aviator to fly solo across the Atlantic Ocean (in 1928). Amelia also published two books, founded an organization for female flyers, became a professor, and became a member of the National Women's Party advocating for the Equal Rights Amendment. She faced her fair share of challenges and opposition. She was often asked why she chose to engage in the dangerous activity of flying. In the movie *Amelia*, a reporter asked her why she wanted to fly. She replied, "Because I want to. I want to be free." When she set out to fly around the world, she was told it could never be done.

My favorite Amelia Earhart quote is, "Never interrupt someone doing what *you* said couldn't be done." Can you imagine how many times she was told that she was crazy, or that she should focus on marriage and children instead of flying? Imagine the media portrayals of her personal goals, and the investors who refused to finance her vision. Imagine the naysayers and critics, and the daily discouragement she must have felt. But Amelia had something more important than the support of the C.A.V.E. people (Citizens Against Virtually Everything)—she believed in herself. She also had her family, who strongly believed in her and consistently encouraged her. Her husband enthusiastically supported her career and cheered her on, and it was her father who took her to the airfield for the very first time and paid $10 for her first flight. These men made a meaningful contribution in her success.

If you are a woman reading this, I want to encourage you to be strong and courageous. If you are a man, I want you to be strong and courageous too! And I hope you will show your strength by supporting the women around you. Support women who run for office. If you're a male candidate, surround yourself with smart women who will make your staff even stronger. As I said in the introduction of this book, I believe we all benefit from diversity of representation. Every group, team, and organization needs people of different genders, races, income levels, personal styles, family histories, educational backgrounds, and more. It is through these different and varied perspectives that we can collaborate to generate better ideas and superior solutions to the challenges that we face together as a society. Wherever your future path takes you, be strong!

I hope the advice, stories, wit, and wisdom I've shared here will aid you in your campaign planning and implementation. But even more, I hope you will move forward with strength and conviction toward whatever vision you have for our political process, our society, and Our World. Whether a candidate or a concerned citizen, I hope that you will set a new standard in politics by engaging in substantive debates. And I hope that you will not be dissuaded from running for office if you feel drawn to that path.

It certainly can be risky to put yourself, your family, and your beliefs and ideas on display in front of the entire world. You will be criticized. You will be challenged. Do it anyway! Run for office anyway! Take a risk, take a stand for what you believe in, build a team, and tackle the impossible. You will be better for it, and so will our political system and Our World.

The Man (or Woman) in the Arena

Excerpt from the speech "Citizenship in a Republic" by Theodore Roosevelt, delivered at the Sorbonne, in Paris, France on April 23, 1910

It is not the critic who counts; not the man who points out how the strong man stumbles, or where the doer of deeds could have done them better. The credit belongs to the man who is actually in the arena, whose face is marred by dust and sweat and blood; who strives valiantly; who errs, who comes up short again and again, because there is no effort without error and shortcoming; but who does actually strive to do the deeds; who knows great enthusiasms, the great devotions; who spends himself in a worthy cause; who at the best knows in the end the triumph of high achievement, and who at the worst, if he fails, at least fails while daring greatly, so that his place shall never be with those cold and timid souls who neither know victory nor defeat.

About the Author

Dr. Casey Lucius is the founder and CEO of Launch Learning Systems in Naples, Florida, a certified woman-owned and veteran-owned small business focusing on strategic planning and team building for government, non-profits, and private industry staffs. From 2008–2016, Lucius and her family lived in California, where she served as a professor of national security decision making at the Naval War College. She was elected to the Pacific Grove City Council from 2012–2016. In 2012, Lucius was certified as an IIMC trainer and began leading strategic planning workshops with local and state agencies. She also offers coaching for political candidates.

Lucius also lived in Hanoi, Vietnam for three years where she served as the Chief of Staff to the US Ambassador at the US Embassy. While in Vietnam, she conducted research and published a book about the political decision-making process. She has published two books and dozens of articles in academic journals, magazines, and online.

Lucius served on active duty as a Naval Intelligence Officer for seven years from 1998–2005. During this time, she earned a master's degree in national security affairs from the Naval Postgraduate School. She deployed to the Middle East on an aircraft carrier, and served at the Pacific Fleet Headquarters in Hawaii as the daily intelligence briefer. While in Hawaii, she utilized the GI Bill and earned a PhD in Political Science from the University of Hawaii.

Dr. Lucius has also worked at the Ohio House of Representatives and the National Association of Manufacturers. She is a graduate of Ashland University and the Naval War College. She is married to Lieutenant Colonel Robert Lucius, USMC (ret). They have one son and too many cats. She can be reached at casey@caseylucius.com.

THE (WO)MAN IN THE ARENA, By Theodore Roosevelt

It is not the critic who counts; not the woman who points out how the strong woman stumbles, or where the doer of deeds could have done them better. The credit belongs to the woman who is actually in the arena, whose face is marred by dust and sweat and blood; who strives valiantly; who errs, who comes short again and again, because there is no effort without error and shortcoming; but who does actually strive to do the deeds; who knows great enthusiasms, the great devotions; who spends herself in a worthy cause; who at the best knows in the end the triumph of high achievement, and who at the worst, if she fails, at least fails while daring greatly, so that her place shall never be with those cold and timid souls who neither know victory nor defeat.

Adapted from the speech "Citizenship in a Republic" delivered at the Sorbonne, in Paris, France on April 23rd, 1910

Image credit to Dennis and Ann Appel